MARY'S MEADOW

AND

OTHER TALES OF FIELDS AND FLOWERS

JULIANA HORATIA EWING

1st WORLD
LIBRARY
Literary Society

Mary's Meadow

Juliana Horatia Ewing

© 1st World Library, 2009
PO Box 2211
Fairfield, IA 52556
www.1stworldlibrary.com
First Edition

LCCN: 2009923475

Softcover ISBN: 978-1-4218-8858-3
Hardcover ISBN: 978-1-4218-8957-3
eBook ISBN: 978-1-4218-8759-3

Purchase *"Mary's Meadow"*
as a traditional bound book at:
www.1stWorldLibrary.com/purchase.asp?ISBN=978-1-4218-8858-3

1ˢᵗ World Library Literary Society

Giving Back to the World

"If you want to work on the core problem, it's early school literacy."

- James Barksdale, former CEO of Netscape

"No skill is more crucial to the future of a child, or to a democratic and prosperous society, than literacy."

- Los Angeles Times

"Literacy... means far more than learning how to read and write... The aim is to transmit... knowledge and promote social participation."

- UNESCO

"Literacy is not a luxury, it is a right and a responsibility. If our world is to meet the challenges of the twenty-first century we must harness the energy and creativity of all our citizens."

- President Bill Clinton

"Parents should be encouraged to read to their children, and teachers should be equipped with all available techniques for teaching literacy, so the varying needs and capacities of individual kids can be taken into account."

- Hugh Mackay

CONTENTS

MARY'S MEADOW 11

LETTERS FROM A LITTLE GARDEN 95

GARDEN LORE.. 124

SUNFLOWERS AND A RUSHLIGHT............... 128

DANDELION CLOCKS 158

THE TRINITY FLOWER...................................... 168

LADDERS TO HEAVEN...................................... 181

MARY'S MEADOW

PREFACE

"MARY'S MEADOW" first appeared in the numbers of *Aunt Judy's Magazine* from November 1883 to March 1884. It was the last serial story which Mrs. EWING wrote, and I believe the subject of it arose from the fact that in 1883, after having spent several years in moving from place to place, she went to live at Villa Ponente, Taunton, where she had a settled home with a garden, and was able to revert to the practical cultivation of flowers, which had been one of the favourite pursuits of her girlhood.

The Game of the Earthly Paradise was received with great delight by the readers of the story; one family of children adopted the word "Mary-meadowing" to describe the work which they did towards beautifying hedges and bare places; and my sister received many letters of inquiry about the various plants mentioned in her tale. These she answered in the correspondence columns of the Magazine, and in July 1884 it was suggested that a "Parkinson Society" should be formed, whose objects were "to search out and cultivate old garden flowers which have become scarce; to exchange seeds and plants; to plant waste places with hardy flowers; to circulate books on gardening amongst the Members;" and further, "to try to prevent the extermination of rare wild flowers, as well as of garden treasures."

Reports of the Society, with correspondence on the exchanges of plants and books, and quaint local names of flowers, were given in the Magazine until it was brought to a close after Mrs. EWING'S death; but I am glad to say that the Society existed for some years under the management of the founder, Miss ALICE SARGANT, and when she was obliged to relinquish the work it was merged in the "Selborne Society," which aims at the preservation of rare species of animals as well as plants.

The "Letters from a Little Garden" were published in *Aunt Judy's Magazine* between November 1884 and February 1885, and as they, as well as "Mary's Meadow," were due to the interest which my sister was taking in the tending of her own Earthly Paradise,—they are inserted in this volume, although they were left unfinished when the writer was called away to be

"Fast in Thy Paradise, where no flower can wither!"

HORATIA K.F. EDEN.

December, 1895.

* * * * *

NOTE.—If any readers of "Mary's Meadow" have been as completely puzzled as the writer was by the title of John Parkinson's old book, it may interest them to know that the question has been raised and answered in *Notes and Queries.*

I first saw the *Paradisi in sole Paradisus terrestris* at Kew, some years ago, and was much bewitched by its quaint charm. I grieve to say that I do not possess it; but an old friend and florist—the Rev. H.T. Ellacombe—was good enough to lend me his copy for reference, and to him I wrote for the meaning of the title. But his scholarship, and that of other learned friends, was quite at fault. My old friend's youthful energies (he will permit me to say that he is ninety-four) were not satisfied to rust in ignorance, and he wrote to *Notes and Queries* on the subject, and has been twice answered. It is an absurd play upon words, after the fashion of John Parkinson's day. Paradise, as *Aunt Judy's* readers may know, is originally an Eastern word, meaning a park, or pleasure-ground. I am ashamed to say that the knowledge of this fact did not help me to the pun. *Paradisi in sole Paradisus terrestris* means Park—in—son's Earthly Paradise!

J.H.E., *February 1884.*

* * * * *

How fresh, O Lord, how sweet and clean
Are Thy returns! ev'n as the flowers in spring;
To which, besides their own demean,
The late-past frosts tributes of pleasure bring.
Grief melts away
Like snow in May,
As if there were no such cold thing.

Who would have thought my shrivel'd heart
Could have recover'd greenness? It was gone
Quite under ground; as flowers depart
To see their mother-root, when they have blown;
Where they together
All the hard weather,
Dead to the world, keep house unknown.

* * * * *

O that I once past changing were,
Fast in Thy Paradise, where no flower can wither!
Many a spring I shoot up fair,
Offering at heaven, growing and groaning thither;
Nor doth my flower
Want a spring-shower,
My sins and I joining together.

*　*　*　*　*

These are Thy wonders, Lord of love,
To make us see we are but flowers that glide:
Which when we once can find and prove,
Thou hast a garden for us, where to bide.
Who would be more,
Swelling through store,
Forfeit their Paradise by their pride.

GEORGE HERBERT.

*　*　*　*　*

CHAPTER I

Mother is always trying to make us love our neighbours as ourselves.

She does so despise us for greediness, or grudging, or snatching, or not sharing what we have got, or taking the best and leaving the rest, or helping ourselves first, or pushing forward, or praising Number One, or being Dogs in the Manger, or anything selfish. And we cannot bear her to despise us!

We despise being selfish, too; but very often we forget. Besides, it is sometimes rather difficult to love your neighbour as yourself when you want a thing very much; and Arthur says he believes it is particularly difficult if it is your next-door-neighbour, and that that is why Father and the Old Squire quarrelled about the footpath through Mary's Meadow.

The Old Squire is not really his name, but that is what people call him. He is very rich. His place comes next to ours, and it is much bigger, and he has quantities of fields, and Father has only got a few; but there are two fields beyond Mary's Meadow which belong to Father, though the Old Squire wanted to buy them. Father would not sell them, and he says he has a right of way through Mary's Meadow to go to his fields, but the Old Squire says he has nothing of the kind, and that is what they quarrelled about.

Arthur says if you quarrel, and are too grown-up to punch each other's heads, you go to law; and if going to law doesn't make it up, you appeal. They went to law, I know, for Mother cried about it; and I suppose it did not make it up, for the Old Squire appealed.

After that he used to ride about all day on his grey horse, with Saxon, his yellow bull-dog, following him, to see that we did not trespass on Mary's Meadow. I think he thought that if we children were there, Saxon would frighten us, for I do not suppose he knew that we knew him. But Saxon used often to come with the Old Squire's Scotch Gardener to see our gardener, and when they were looking at the wall-fruit, Saxon used to come snuffing after us.

He is the nicest dog I know. He looks very savage, but he is only very funny. His lower jaw sticks out, which makes him grin, and some people think he is gnashing his teeth with rage. We think it looks as if he were laughing—like Mother Hubbard's dog, when she brought home his coffin, and he wasn't dead—but it really is only the shape of his jaw. I loved Saxon the first day I saw him, and he likes me, and licks my face. But what he likes best of all are Bath Oliver Biscuits.

One day the Scotch Gardener saw me feeding him, and he pulled his red beard, and said, "Ye do weel to mak' hay while the sun shines, Saxon, my man. There's sma' sight o' young leddies and sweet cakes at hame for ye!" And Saxon grinned, and wagged his tail, and the Scotch Gardener touched his hat to me, and took him away.

The Old Squire's Weeding Woman is our nursery-maid's

Juliana Horatia Ewing

aunt. She is not very old, but she looks so, because she has lost her teeth, and is bent nearly double. She wears a large hood, and carries a big basket, which she puts down outside the nursery door when she comes to tea with Bessy. If it is a fine afternoon, and we are gardening, she lets us borrow the basket, and then we play at being weeding women in each other's gardens.

She tells Bessy about the Old Squire. She says—"He do be a real old skinflint, the Old Zquire a be!" But she thinks it— "zim as if 'twas having ne'er a wife nor child for to keep the natur' in 'un, so his heart do zim to shrivel, like they walnuts Butler tells us of as a zets down for desart. The Old Zquire he mostly eats ne'er a one now's teeth be so bad. But a counts them every night when's desart's done. And a keeps 'em till the karnels be mowldy, and a keeps 'em till they be dry, and a keeps 'em till they be dust; and when the karnels is dust, a cracks aal the lot of 'em when desart's done, zo's no one mayn't have no good of they walnuts, since they be no good to be."

Arthur can imitate the Weeding Woman exactly, and he can imitate the Scotch Gardener too. Chris (that is Christopher, our youngest brother) is very fond of "The Zquire and the Walnuts." He gets nuts, or anything, like shells or bits of flower-pots, that will break, and something to hit with, and when Arthur comes to "*The karnels is dust,*" Chris smashes everything before him, shouting, "*A cracks aal the lot of em,*" and then he throws the bits all over the place, with "*They be no good to he.*"

Father laughed very much when he heard Arthur do the Weeding Woman, and Mother could not help laughing too; but she did not like it, because she does not like us to repeat servants' gossip.

The Weeding Woman is a great gossip. She gossips all the time she is having her tea, and it is generally about the Old Squire. She used to tell Bessy that his flowers bloomed themselves to death, and the fruit rotted on the walls, because he would let nothing be picked, and gave nothing away, except now and then a grand present of fruit to Lady Catherine, for which the old lady returned no thanks, but only a rude message to say that his peaches were over-ripe, and he had better have sent the grapes to the Infirmary. Adela asked—"Why is the Old Squire so kind to Lady Catherine?" and Father said—"Because we are so fond of Lords and Ladies in this part of the country." I thought he meant the lords and ladies in the hedges, for we are very fond of them. But he didn't. He meant real lords and ladies.

There are splendid lords and ladies in the hedges of Mary's Meadow. I never can make up my mind when I like them best. In April and May, when they have smooth plum-coloured coats and pale green cowls, and push up out of last year's dry leaves, or in August and September, when their hoods have fallen away, and their red berries shine through the dusty grass and nettles that have been growing up round them all the summer out of the ditch.

Flowers were one reason for our wanting to go to Mary's Meadow. Another reason was the nightingale. There was one that used always to sing there, and Mother had made us a story about it.

We are very fond of fairy books, and one of our greatest favourites is Bechstein's *As Pretty as Seven*. It has very nice pictures, and we particularly like "The Man in the Moon, and How He Came There;" but the story doesn't end well, for he came there by gathering sticks on Sunday, and then scoffing about it, and he has been there ever since. But Mother made us a new fairy tale about the nightingale in Mary's Meadow

Juliana Horatia Ewing

being the naughty woodcutter's only child, who was turned into a little brown bird that lives on in the woods, and sits on a tree on summer nights, and sings to its father up in the moon.

But after our Father and the Old Squire went to law, Mother told us we must be content with hearing the nightingale from a distance. We did not really know about the lawsuit then, we only understood that the Old Squire was rather crosser than usual; and we rather resented being warned not to go into Mary's Meadow, especially as Father kept saying we had a perfect right so to do. I thought that Mother was probably afraid of Saxon being set at us, and of course I had no fears about him. Indeed, I used to wish that it could happen that the Old Squire, riding after me as full of fury as King Padella in the *Rose and the Ring*, might set Saxon on me, as the lions were let loose to eat the Princess Rosalba. "Instead of devouring her with their great teeth, it was with kisses they gobbled her up. They licked her pretty feet, they nuzzled their noses in her lap," and she put her arms "round their tawny necks and kissed them." Saxon gobbles us with kisses, and nuzzles his nose, and we put our arms round his tawny neck. What a surprise it would be to the Old Squire to see him! And then I wondered if my feet were as pretty as Rosalba's, and I thought they were, and I wondered if Saxon would lick them, supposing that by any possibility it could ever happen that I should be barefoot in Mary's Meadow at the mercy of the Old Squire and his bull-dog.

One does not, as a rule, begin to go to bed by letting down one's hair, and taking off one's shoes and stockings. But one night I was silly enough to do this, just to see if I looked (in the mirror) at all like the picture of Rosalba in the *Rose and the Ring*. I was trying to see my feet as well as my hair, when I heard Arthur jumping the three steps in the middle of the passage between his room and mine. I had only just time to spring into the window-seat, and tuck my feet under me, when he gave a hasty knock, and bounced in with his telescope in his hand.

"Oh, Mary," he cried, "I want you to see the Old Squire, with a great-coat over his evening clothes, and a squash hat, marching up and down Mary's Meadow."

And he pulled up my blind, and threw open the window, and arranged the telescope for me.

It was a glorious night. The moon was rising round and large out of the mist, and dark against its brightness I could see the figure of the Old Squire pacing the pathway over Mary's Meadow.

Saxon was not there; but on a slender branch of a tree in the hedgerow sat the nightingale, singing to comfort the poor, lonely old Man in the Moon.

Juliana Horatia Ewing

CHAPTER II

Lady Catherine is Mother's aunt by marriage, and Mother is one of the few people she is not rude to.

She is very rude, and yet she is very kind, especially to the poor. But she does kind things so rudely, that people now and then wish that she would mind her own business instead. Father says so, though Mother would say that that is gossip. But I think sometimes that Mother is thinking of Aunt Catherine when she tells us that in kindness it is not enough to be good to others, one should also learn to be gracious.

Mother thought she was very rude to *her* once, when she said, quite out loud, that Father is very ill-tempered, and that, if Mother had not the temper of an angel, the house could never hold together. Mother was very angry, but Father did not mind. He says our house will hold together much longer than most houses, because he swore at the workmen, and went to law with the builder for using dirt instead of mortar, so the builder had to pull down what was done wrong, and do it right; and Father says he knows he has a bad temper, but he does not mean to pull the house over our heads at present, unless he has to get bricks out to heave at Lady Catherine if she becomes quite unbearable.

We do not like dear Father to be called bad-tempered. He

comes home cross sometimes, and then we have to be very quiet, and keep out of the way; and sometimes he goes out rather cross, but not always. It was what Chris said about that that pleased Lady Catherine so much.

It was one day when Father came home cross, and was very much vexed to find us playing about the house. Arthur had got a new Adventure Book, and he had been reading to us about the West Coast of Africa, and niggers, and tom-toms, and "going Fantee;" and James gave him a lot of old corks out of the pantry, and let him burn them in a candle. It rained, and we could not go out; so we all blacked our faces with burnt cork, and played at the West Coast in one of the back passages, and at James being the captain of a slave ship, because he tried to catch us when we beat the tom-toms too near him when he was cleaning the plate, to make him give us rouge and whitening to tattoo with.

Dear Father came home rather earlier than we expected, and rather cross. Chris did not hear the front door, because his ears were pinched up with tying curtain rings on to them, and just at that minute he shouted, "I go Fantee!" and tore his pinafore right up the middle, and burst into the front hall with it hanging in two pieces by the armholes, his eyes shut, and a good grab of James's rouge-powder smudged on his nose, yelling and playing the tom-tom on what is left of Arthur's drum.

Father was very angry indeed, and Chris was sent to bed, and not allowed to go down to dessert; and Lady Catherine was dining at our house, so he missed her.

Next time she called, and saw Chris, she asked him why he had not been at dessert that night. Mother looked at Chris, and said, "Why was it, Chris? Tell Aunt Catherine." Mother thought he would say, "Because I tore my pinafore, and made a noise in the front hall." But he smiled, the grave way Chris does, and said, "Because Father came home cross." And Lady Catherine was pleased, but Mother was vexed.

I am quite sure Chris meant no harm, but he does say very funny things. Perhaps it is because his head is rather large for his body, with some water having got into his brain when he was very little, so that we have to take care of him. And though he does say very odd things, very slowly, I do not think any one of us tries harder to be good.

I remember once Mother had been trying to make us forgive each other's trespasses, and Arthur would say that you cannot *make* yourself feel kindly to them that trespass against you; and Mother said if you make yourself do right, then at last you get to feel right; and it was very soon after this that Harry and Christopher quarrelled, and would not forgive each other's trespasses in the least, in spite of all that I could do to try and make peace between them.

Chris went off in the sulks, but after a long time I came upon him in the toy-cupboard, looking rather pale and very large-headed, and winding up his new American top, and talking to himself.

When he talks to himself he mutters, so I could only just hear what he was saying, and he said it over and over again:

"*Dos first and feels afterwards.*"

"What are you doing, Chris?" I asked.

"I'm getting ready my new top to give to Harry. *Dos first and feels afterwards.*"

"Well," I said, "Christopher, you *are* a good boy."

"I should like to punch his head," said Chris—and he said it in just the same sing-song tone—"but I'm getting the top ready. *Dos first and feels afterwards*."

And he went on winding and muttering.

Afterwards he told me that the "feels" came sooner than he expected. Harry wouldn't take his top, and they made up their quarrel.

Christopher is very simple, but sometimes we think he is also a little sly. He can make very wily excuses about things he does not like.

He does not like Nurse to hold back his head and wash his face; and at last one day she let him go down-stairs with a dirty face, and then complained to Mother. So Mother asked Chris why he was so naughty about having his face washed, and he said, quite gravely, "I do think it would be *such pity* if the water got into my head again by accident." Mother did not know he had ever heard about it, but she said, "Oh, Chris! Chris! that's one of your excuses." And he said, "It's not my *'scusis*. She lets a good deal get in—at my ears—and lather too."

But, with all his whimsical ways, Lady Catherine is devoted to Christopher. She likes him far better than any one of us, and he is very fond of her; and they say quite rude things to each other all along. And Father says it is very lucky, for if she had not been so fond of Chris, and so ready to take him too, Mother would never have been persuaded to leave us when Aunt Catherine took them to the South of France.

Mother had been very unwell for a long time. She has so many worries, and Dr. Solomon said she ought to avoid worry, and Aunt Catherine said worries were killing her, and

Father said "Pshaw!" and Aunt Catherine said "Care killed the cat," and that a cat has nine lives, and a woman has only one; and then Mother got worse, and Aunt Catherine wanted to take her abroad, and she wouldn't go; and then Christopher was ill, and Aunt Catherine said she would take him too, if only Mother would go with her; and Dr. Solomon said it might be the turning-point of his health, and Father said "the turning-point which way?" but he thanked Lady Catherine, and they didn't quarrel; and so Mother yielded, and it was settled that they should go.

Before they went, Mother spoke to me, and told me I must be a Little Mother to the others whilst she was away. She hoped we should all try to please Father, and to be unselfish with each other; but she expected me to try far harder than the others, and never to think of myself at all, so that I might fill her place whilst she was away. So I promised to try, and I did.

We missed Christopher sadly. And Saxon missed him. The first time Saxon came to see us after Mother and Chris went away, we told him all about it, and he looked very sorry. Then we said that he should be our brother in Christopher's stead, whilst Chris was away; and he looked very much pleased, and wagged his tail, and licked our faces all round. So we told him to come and see us very often.

He did not, but we do not think it was his fault. He is chained up so much.

One day Arthur and I were walking down the road outside the Old Squire's stables, and Saxon smelt us, and we could hear him run and rattle his chain, and he gave deep, soft barks.

Arthur laughed. He said, "Do you hear Saxon, Mary? Now I

dare say the Old Squire thinks he smells tramps and wants to bite them. He doesn't know that Saxon smells his new sister and brother, and wishes he could go out walking with them in Mary's Meadow."

Juliana Horatia Ewing

CHAPTER III

Nothing comforted us so much whilst Mother and Chris were away as being allowed to play in the library.

We were not usually allowed to be there so often, but when we asked Father he gave us leave to amuse ourselves there at the time when Mother would have had us with her, provided that we did not bother him or hurt the books. We did not hurt the books, and in the end we were allowed to go there as much as we liked.

We have plenty of books of our own, and we have new ones very often: on birthdays and at Christmas. Sometimes they are interesting, and sometimes they are disappointing. Most of them have pretty pictures. It was because we had been rather unlucky for some time, and had had disappointing ones on our birthdays, that Arthur said to me, "Look here, Mary, I'm not going to read any books now but grown-up ones, unless it is an Adventure Book. I'm sick of books for young people, there's so much *stuff* in them."

We call it *stuff* when there seems to be going to be a story and it comes to nothing but talk; and we call it *stuff* when there is a very interesting picture, and you read to see what it is about, and the reading does not tell you, or tells you wrong.

Both Arthur and Christopher had had disappointments in their books on their birthdays.

Arthur jumped at his book at first, because there were Japanese pictures in it, and Uncle Charley had just been staying with us, and had brought beautiful Japanese pictures with him, and had told us Japanese fairy tales, and they were as good as Bechstein. So Arthur was full of Japan.

The most beautiful picture of all was of a stork, high up in a tall pine tree, and the branches of the pine tree, and the cones, and the pine needles were most beautifully drawn; and there was a nest with young storks in it, and behind the stork and the nest and the tall pine the sun was blazing with all his rays. And Uncle Charley told us the story to it, and it was called "the Nest of the Stork."

So when Arthur saw a stork standing among pine needles in his new book he shouted with delight, though the pine needles were rather badly done, with thick strokes. But presently he said, "It's not nearly so good a stork as Uncle Charley's. And where's the stem of the pine? It looks as if the stork were on the ground and on the top of the pine tree too, and there's no nest. And there's no sun. And, oh! Mary, what do you think is written under it? *Crane and Water-reeds.*' Well, I do call that a sell!"

Christopher's disappointment was quite as bad. Mother gave him a book with very nice pictures, particularly of beasts. The chief reason she got it for him was that there was such a very good picture of a toad, and Chris is so fond of toads. For months he made friends with one in the garden. It used to crawl away from him, and he used to creep after it, talking to it, and then it used to half begin, to crawl up the garden wall, and stand so, on its hind legs, and let Chris rub its wrinkled back. The toad in the picture was exactly like

Juliana Horatia Ewing

Christopher's toad, and he ran about the house with the book in his arms begging us to read him the story about Dear Toady.

We were all busy but Arthur, and he said, "I want to go on with my water-wheel." But Mother said, "Don't be selfish, Arthur." And he said, "I forgot. All right, Chris; bring me the book." So they went and sat in the conservatory, not to disturb any one. But very soon they came back, Chris crying, and saying, "It couldn't be the right one, Arthur;" and Arthur frowning, and saying, "It *is* the right story; but it's *stuff*. I'll tell you what that book's good for, Chris. To paint the pictures. And you've got a new paint-box." So Mother said, "What's the matter?" And Arthur said, "Chris thinks I haven't read him the right story to his Toad Picture. But I have, and what do you think it's about? It's about the silliest little girl you can imagine—a regular mawk of a girl—*and a Frog*. Not a toad, but a F. R. O. G. frog! A regular hop, skip, jumping frog!"

Arthur hopped round the room, but Chris cried bitterly. So Arthur ran up to him and kissed him, and said, "Don't cry, old chap, I'll tell you what I'll do. You get Mary to cut out a lot of the leaves of your book that have no pictures, and that will make it like a real scrap-book; and then I'll give you a lot of my scraps and pictures to paste over what's left of the stories, and you'll have such a painting-book as you never had in all your life before."

So we did. And Arthur was very good, for he gave Chris pictures that I know he prized, because Chris liked them. But the very first picture he gave him was the "Crane and Water-reeds."

I thought it so good of Arthur to be so nice with Chris that I wished I could have helped him over his water-wheel. He had put Japan out of his head since the disappointment, and spent all his play-time in making mills and machinery. He did grind some corn into flour once, but it was not at all white. He said that was because the bran was left in. But it was not only bran in Arthur's flour. There was a good deal of sand too, from his millstones being made of sandstone, which he thought would not matter. But it grinds off.

Down in the valley, below Mary's Meadow, runs the Ladybrook, which turns the old water-wheel of Mary's Mill. It is a very picturesque old mill, and Mother has made beautyful sketches of it. She caught the last cold she got before going abroad with sketching it—the day we had a most delightful picnic there, and went about in the punt. And from that afternoon Arthur made up his mind that his next mill should be a water-mill.

The reason I am no good at helping Arthur about his mills is that I am stupid about machinery; and I was so vexed not to help him, that when I saw a book in the library which I thought would do so, I did not stop to take it out, for it was in four very large volumes, but ran off at once to tell Arthur.

He said, "What *is* the matter, Mary?"

I said, "Oh, Arthur! I've found a book that will tell you all about mills; and it is the nicest smelling book in the library."

"The nicest *smelling*? What's that got to do with mills?"

"Nothing, of course. But it's bound in russia, and I am so fond of the smell of russia. But that's nothing. It's a Miller's Dictionary, and it is in four huge volumes, 'with plates.' I should think you could look out all about every kind of mill there ever was a miller to."

Juliana Horatia Ewing

"If the plates give sections and diagrams"—Arthur began, but I did not hear the rest, for he started off for the library at once, and I ran after him.

But when we got Miller's Dictionary on the floor, how he did tease me! For there was nothing about mills or millers in it. It was a Gardener's and Botanist's Dictionary, by Philip Miller; and the plates were plates of flowers, very truly drawn, like the pine tree in Uncle Charley's Jap. picture. There were some sections too, but they were sections of greenhouses, not of any kinds of mills or machinery.

The odd thing was that it turned out a kind of help to Arthur after all. For we got so much interested in it that it roused us up about our gardens. We are all very fond of flowers, I most of all. And at last Arthur said he thought that miniature mills were really rather humbugging things, and it would be much easier and more useful to build a cold frame to keep choice auriculas and *half-hardies* in.

When we took up our gardens so hotly, Harry and Adela took up theirs, and we did a great deal, for the weather was fine.

We were surprised to find that the Old Squire's Scotch Gardener knew Miller's Gardener's Dictionary quite well. He said, "It's a gran' wurrk!" (Arthur can say it just like him.)

One day he wished he could see it, and smell the russia binding; he said he liked to feel a nice smell. Father was away, and we were by ourselves, so we invited him into the library. Saxon wanted to come in too, but the gardener was very cross with him, and sent him out; and he sat on the mat outside and dribbled with longing to get in, and thudded his stiff tail whenever he saw any one through the doorway.

The Scotch Gardener enjoyed himself very much, and he explained a lot of things to Arthur, and helped us to put away the Dictionary when we had done with it.

When he took up his hat to go, he gave one long look all round the library. Then he turned to Arthur (and Saxon took advantage of this to wag his way in and join the party), and said, "It's a rare privilege, the free entry of a book chamber like this. I'm hoping, young gentleman, that you're not insensible of it?"

Then he caught sight of Saxon, and beat him out of the room with his hat.

But he came back himself to say, that it might just happen that he would be glad now and again to hear what was said about this or that plant (of which he would write down the botanical name) in these noble volumes.

So we told him that if he would bring Saxon to see us pretty often, we would look out anything he wanted to know about in Miller's Gardener's Dictionary.

CHAPTER IV

Looking round the library one day, to see if I could see any more books about gardening, I found the Book of Paradise.

It is a very old book, and very queer. It has a brown leather back—not russia—and stiff little gold flowers and ornaments all the way down, where Miller's Dictionary has gold swans in crowns, and ornaments.

There are a good many old books in the library, but they are not generally very interesting—at least not to us. So when I found that though this one had a Latin name on the title-page, it was written in English, and that though it seemed to be about Paradise, it was really about a garden, and quite common flowers, I was delighted, for I always have cared more for gardening and flowers than for any other amusement, long before we found Miller's Gardener's Dictionary. And the Book of Paradise is much smaller than the Dictionary, and easier to hold. And I like old, queer things, and it is very old and queer.

The Latin name is *Paradisi in sole, Paradisus terrestris*, which we do not any of us understand, though we are all learning Latin; so we call it the Book of Paradise. But the English name is—"Or a Garden of all sorts of pleasant flowers which our English ayre will permitt to be noursed up;" and on the top of every page is written "The Garden of Pleasant Flowers," and it says—"Collected by John Parkinson, Apothecary of London, and the King's Herbarist, 1629."

I had to think a minute to remember who was the king then, and it was King Charles I.; so then I knew that it was Queen Henrietta to whom the book was dedicated. This was the dedication:—

"TO THE QUEEN'S MOST EXCELLENT MAJESTY.

"MADAME,—Knowing your Majesty so much delighted with all the fair flowers of a Garden, and furnished with them as far beyond others as you are eminent before them; this my Work of a Garden long before this intended to be published, and but now only finished, seemed as it were destined to be first offered into your Highness's hands as of right, challenging the propriety of Patronage from all others. Accept, I beseech your Majesty, this speaking Garden, that may inform you in all the particulars of your store as well as wants, when you cannot see any of them fresh upon the ground: and it shall further encourage him to accomplish the remainder; who in praying that your Highness may enjoy the heavenly Paradise, after many years' fruition of this earthly, submitteth to be your Majesties,

"In all humble devotion,

"JOHN PARKINSON."

We like queer old things like this, they are so funny! I liked the Dedication, and I wondered if the Queen's Garden really was an Earthly Paradise, and whether she did enjoy reading John Parkinson's book about flowers in the winter time, when her own flowers were no longer "fresh upon the ground." And then I wondered what flowers she had, and I looked out a great many of our chief favourites, and she had several kinds of them.

We are particularly fond of Daffodils, and she had several kinds of Daffodils, from the "Primrose Peerlesse,"[1] "of a sweet but stuffing scent," to "the least Daffodil of all,"[2] which the book says "was brought to us by a Frenchman called Francis le Vean, the honestest root-gatherer that ever came over to us."

[Footnote 1: *Narcissus media lutens vulgaris.*]

[Footnote 2: *Narcissus minimus*, Parkinson. *N. minor*, Miller.]

The Queen had Cowslips too, though our gardener despised them when he saw them in my garden. I dug mine up in Mary's Meadow before Father and the Old Squire went to law; but they were only common Cowslips, with one Oxlip, by good luck. In the Earthly Paradise there were "double Cowslips, one within another." And they were called Hose-in-Hose. I wished I had Hose-in-Hose.

Arthur was quite as much delighted with the Book of Paradise as I. He said, "Isn't it funny to think of Queen Henrietta Maria gardening! I wonder if she went trailing up and down the walks looking like that picture of her we saw when you and I were in London with Mother about our teeth, and went to see the Loan Collection of Old Masters. I wonder if the Dwarf picked the flowers for her. I do wonder what Apothecary John Parkinson looked like when he offered his Speaking Garden into her Highness's hands. And what beautiful hands she had! Do you remember the picture, Mary? It was by Vandyck."

I remembered it quite well.

That afternoon the others could not amuse themselves, and wanted me to tell them a story. They do not like old stories too often, and it is rather difficult to invent new ones. Sometimes we do it by turns. We sit in a circle and one of us begins, and the next must add something, and so we go on. But that way does not make a good plot. My head was so full of the Book of Paradise that afternoon that I could not think of a story, but I said I would begin one. So I began:

"Once upon a time there was a Queen—"

"How was she dressed?" asked Adela, who thinks a good deal about dress.

"She had a beautiful dark-blue satin robe."

"*Princesse* shape?" inquired Adela.

"No; Queen's shape," said Arthur. "Drive on, Mary."

"And lace ruffles falling back from her Highness's hands—"

"Sweet!" murmured Adela.

"And a high hat, with plumes, on her head, and—"

"A very low dwarf at her heels," added Arthur.

"Was there really a dwarf, Mary?" asked Harry.

"There was," said I.

"Had he a hump, or was he only a plain dwarf?"

"He was a very plain dwarf," said Arthur.

"Does Arthur know the story, Mary?"

"No, Harry, he doesn't; and he oughtn't to interfere till I come to a stop."

"Beg pardon, Mary. Drive on."

"The Queen was very much delighted with all fair flowers, and she had a garden so full of them that it was called the Earthly Paradise."

There was a long-drawn and general "Oh!" of admiration.

"But though she was a Queen, she couldn't have flowers in the winter, not even in an Earthly Paradise."

"Don't you suppose she had a greenhouse, by the bye, Mary?" said Arthur.

"Oh, Arthur," cried Harry, "I do wish you'd be quiet: when you know it's a fairy story, and that Queens of that sort never had greenhouses or anything like we have now."

"And so the King's Apothecary and Herbarist, whose name was John Parkinson—"

"I shouldn't have thought he would have had a common name like that," said Harry.

"Bessy's name is Parkinson," said Adela.

"Well, I can't help it; his name *was* John Parkinson."

"Drive on, Mary!" said Arthur.

"And he made her a book, called the Book of Paradise, in which there were pictures and written accounts of her flowers, so that when she could not see any of them fresh upon the ground, she could read about them, and think about them, and count up how many she had."

"Ah, but she couldn't tell. Some of them might have died in the winter," said Adela.

"Ah, but some of the others might have got little ones at their roots," said Harry. "So that would make up."

I said nothing. I was glad of the diversion, for I could not think how to go on with the story. Before I quite gave in, Harry luckily asked, "Was there a Weeding Woman in the Earthly Paradise?"

"There was," said I.

"How was she dressed?" asked Adela.

"She had a dress the colour of common earth."

"*Princesse* shape?" inquired Arthur.

"No; Weeding Woman shape. Arthur, I wish you wouldn't—"

"All right, Mary. Drive on."

"And a little shawl, that had partly the colour of grass, and partly the colour of hay."

"*Hay dear!*" interpolated Arthur, exactly imitating a well-known sigh peculiar to Bessy's aunt.

"Was her bonnet like our Weeding Woman's bonnet?" asked

Adela, in a disappointed tone.

"Much larger," said I, "and the colour of a Marigold."

Adela looked happier. "Strings the same?" she asked.

"No. One string canary-colour, and the other white."

"And a basket?" asked Harry.

"Yes, a basket, of course. Well, the Queen had all sorts of flowers in her garden. Some of them were natives of the country, and some of them were brought to her from countries far away, by men called Root-gatherers. There were very beautiful Daffodils in the Earthly Paradise, but the smallest of all the Daffodils—"

"A Dwarf, like the Hunchback?" said Harry.

"The Dwarf Daffodil of all was brought to her by a man called Francis le Vean."

"That was a *much* nicer name than John Parkinson," said Harry.

"And he was the honestest Root-gatherer that ever brought foreign flowers into the Earthly Paradise."

"Then I love him!" said Harry.

CHAPTER V

One sometimes thinks it is very easy to be good, and then there comes something which makes it very hard.

I liked being a Little Mother to the others, and almost enjoyed giving way to them. "Others first, Little Mothers afterwards," as we used to say—till the day I made up that story for them out of the Book of Paradise.

The idea of it took our fancy completely, the others as well as mine, and though the story was constantly interrupted, and never came to any real plot or end, there were no Queens, or dwarfs, or characters of any kind in all Bechstein's fairy tales, or even in Grimm, more popular than the Queen of the Blue Robe and her Dwarf, and the Honest Root-gatherer, and John Parkinson, King's Apothecary and Herbarist, and the Weeding Woman of the Earthly Paradise.

When I said, "Wouldn't it be a good new game to have an Earthly Paradise in our gardens, and to have a King's Apothecary and Herbarist to gather things and make medicine of them, and an Honest Root-gatherer to divide the polyanthus plants and the bulbs when we take them up, and divide them fairly, and a Weeding Woman to work and make things tidy, and a Queen in a blue dress, and Saxon for the Dwarf"—the others set up such a shout of approbation that

Juliana Horatia Ewing

Father sent James to inquire if we imagined that he was going to allow his house to be turned into a bear-garden.

And Arthur said, "No. Tell him we're only turning it into a Speaking Garden, and we're going to turn our own gardens into an Earthly Paradise."

But I said, "Oh, James! please don't say anything of the kind. Say we're very sorry, and we will be quite quiet."

And James said, "Trust me, Miss. It would be a deal more than my place is worth to carry Master Arthur's messages to his Pa."

"I'll be the Honestest Root-gatherer," said Harry. "I'll take up Dandelion roots to the very bottom, and sell them to the King's Apothecary to make Dandelion tea of."

"That's a good idea of yours, Harry," said Arthur. "I shall be John Parkinson—"

"*My* name is Francis le Vean," said Harry.

"King's Apothecary and Herbarist," continued Arthur, disdaining the interruption. "And I'll bet you my Cloth of Gold Pansy to your Black Prince that Bessy's aunt takes three bottles of my dandelion and camomile mixture for 'the swimmings,' bathes her eyes every morning with my elder-flower lotion to strengthen the sight, and sleeps every night on my herb pillow (if Mary'll make me a flannel bag) before the week's out."

"I could make you a flannel bag," said Adela, "if Mary will make me a bonnet, so that I can be the Weeding Woman. You could make it of tissue-paper, with stiff paper inside, like all those caps you made for us last Christmas, Mary dear, couldn't you? And there is some lovely orange-coloured paper, I know, and pale yellow, and white. The bonnet was Marigold colour, was it not? And one string canary-coloured and one white. I couldn't tie them, of course, being paper; but Bessy's aunt doesn't tie her bonnet. She wears it like a helmet, to shade her eyes. I shall wear mine so too. It will be all Marigold, won't it, dear? Front *and* crown; and the white string going back over one shoulder and the canary string over the other. They might be pinned together behind, perhaps, if they were in my way. Don't you think so?"

I said "Yes," because if one does not say something, Adela never stops saying whatever it is she is saying, even if she has to say it two or three times over.

But I felt so cross and so selfish, that if Mother *could* have known she *would* have despised me!

For the truth was, I had set my heart upon being the Weeding Woman. I thought Adela would want to be the Queen, because of the blue dress, and the plumed hat, and the lace ruffles. Besides, she likes picking flowers, but she never liked grubbing. She would not really like the Weeding Woman's work; it was the bonnet that had caught her fancy, and I found it hard to smother the vexing thought that if I had gone on dressing the Weeding Woman of the Earthly Paradise like Bessy's aunt, instead of trying to make the story more interesting by inventing a marigold bonnet with yellow and white strings for her, I might have had the part I wished to play in our new game (which certainly was of my devising), and Adela would have been better pleased to be the Queen than to be anything else.

As it was, I knew that if I asked her she would give up the Weeding Woman. Adela is very good, and she is very

Juliana Horatia Ewing

good-natured. And I knew, too, that it would not have cost her much. She would have given a sigh about the bonnet, and then have turned her whole attention to a blue robe, and how to manage the ruffles.

But even whilst I was thinking about it, Arthur said: "Of course, Mary must be the Queen, unless we could think of something else—very good—for her. If we could have thought of something, Mary, I was thinking how jolly it would be, when Mother comes home, to have had *her* for the Queen, with Chris for her Dwarf, and to give her flowers out of our Earthly Paradise."

"She would, look just like a Queen," said Harry.

"In her navy blue nun's cloth and Russian lace," said Adela.

That settled the question. Nothing could be so nice as to have Mother in the game, and the plan provided for Christopher also. I had no wish to be Queen, as far as that went. Dressing up, and walking about the garden would be no fun for me. I really had looked forward to clearing away big baskets full of weeds and rubbish, and keeping our five gardens and the paths between them so tidy as they had never been kept before. And I knew the weeds would have a fine time of it with Adela, as Weeding Woman, in a tissue-paper bonnet!

But one thing was more important, than tidy gardens—not to be selfish.

I had been left as Little Mother to the others, and I had been lucky enough to think of a game that pleased them. If I turned selfish now, it would spoil everything.

So I said that Arthur's idea was excellent; that I had no wish to be Queen, that I thought I might, perhaps, devise another character for myself by and by; and that if the others would leave me alone, I would think about it whilst I was making Adela's bonnet.

The others were quite satisfied. Father says people always are satisfied with things in general, when they've got what they want for themselves, and I think that is true.

I got the tissue-paper and the gum; resisted Adela's extreme desire to be with me and talk about the bonnet, and shut myself up in the library.

I got out the Book of Paradise too, and propped it up in an arm-chair, and sat on a footstool in front of it, so that I could read in between whiles of making the bonnet. There is an index, so that you can look out the flowers you want to read about. It was no use our looking out flowers, except common ones, such as Harry would be allowed to get bits of out of the big garden to plant in our little gardens, when he became our Honest Root-gatherer.

I looked at the Cowslips again. I am very fond of them, and so, they say, are nightingales; which is, perhaps, why that nightingale we know lives in Mary's Meadow, for it is full of cowslips.

The Queen had a great many kinds, and there are pictures of most of them. She had the Common Field Cowslip, the Primrose Cowslip, the Single Green Cowslip, Curled Cowslips, or Galligaskins, Double Cowslips, or Hose-in-Hose, and the Franticke or Foolish Cowslip, or Jackanapes on Horsebacke.

I did not know one of them except the Common Cowslip, but I remembered that Bessy's aunt once told me that she had a double cowslip. It was the day I was planting common ones in my garden, when our gardener despised them. Bessy's aunt despised them too, and she said the double ones were only fit for a cottage garden. I laughed so much that I tore the canary-coloured string as I was gumming it on to the bonnet, to think how I could tell her now that cowslips are Queen's flowers, the common ones as well as the Hose-in-Hose.

Then I looked out the Honeysuckle, it was page 404, and there were no pictures. I began at the beginning of the chapter; this was it, and it was as funnily spelt as the preface, but I could read it.

"Chap. cv. *Periclymemum*. Honeysuckles.

"The Honisucle that groweth wilde in euery hedge, although it be very sweete, yet doe I not bring it into my garden, but let it rest in his owne place, to serue their senses that trauell by it, or haue no garden."

I had got so far when James came in. He said—"Letters, miss."

It was the second post, and there was a letter for me, and a book parcel; both from Mother.

Mother's letters are always delightful; and, like things she says, they often seem to come in answer to something you have been thinking about, and which you would never imagine she could know, unless she was a witch. This was *the knowing bit* in that letter:—"*Your dear father's note this morning did me more good than bottles of tonic. It is due to you, my trust-worthy little daughter, to tell you of the bit that pleased me most. He says—'The children seem to me to be behaving unusually well, and I must say, I believe the credit belongs to Mary. She seems to have a genius for keeping them amused, which luckily means keeping them out of* mischief.' Now, good Little Mother, I wonder how you yourself are being entertained? I hope the others are not presuming on your unselfishness? Anyhow, I send you a book for your own amusement when they leave you a bit of peace and quiet. I have long been fond of it in French, and I have found an English translation with nice little pictures, and send it to you. I know you will enjoy it, because you are so fond of flowers."

Oh, how glad I was that I had let Adela be the Weeding Woman with a good grace, and could open my book parcel with a clear conscience!

I put the old book away and buried myself in the new one.

I never had a nicer. It was called *A Tour Round my Garden*, and some of the little stories in it—like the Tulip Rebecca, and the Discomfited Florists—were very amusing indeed; and some were sad and pretty, like the Yellow Roses; and there were delicious bits, like the Enriched Woodman and the Connoisseur Deceived; but there was no "stuff" in it at all.

Some chapters were duller than others, and at last I got into a very dull one, about the vine, and it had a good deal of Greek in it, and we have not begun Greek.

But after the Greek, and the part about Bacchus and Anacreon (I did not care about *them*; they were not in the least like the Discomfited Florists, or the Enriched Woodman!) there came this, and I liked it the best of all:—

"At the extremity of my garden the vine extends in long porticoes, through the arcades of which may be seen trees of all sorts, and foliage of all colours. There is an *azerolier* (a small medlar) which is covered in autumn with little apples, producing the richest effect. I have given away several grafts of this; far from deriving pleasure from the privation of others, I do my utmost to spread and render common and vulgar all the trees and plants that I prefer; it is as if I multiplied the pleasure and the chances of beholding them of all who, like me, really love flowers for their splendour, their grace, and their perfume. Those who, on the contrary, are jealous of their plants, and only esteem them in proportion with their conviction that no one else possesses them, do not love flowers; and be assured that it is either chance or poverty which has made them collectors of flowers, instead of being collectors of pictures, cameos, medals, or any other thing that might serve as an excuse for indulging in all the joys of possession, seasoned with the idea that others do not possess.

"I have even carried the vulgarization of beautiful flowers farther than this.

"I ramble about the country near my dwelling, and seek the wildest and least-frequented spots. In these, after clearing and preparing a few inches of ground, I scatter the seeds of my most favourite plants, which re-sow themselves, per-petuate themselves, and multiply themselves. At this moment, whilst the fields display nothing but the common red poppy, strollers find with surprise in certain wild nooks of our country, the most beautiful double poppies, with their white, red, pink, carnation, and variegated blossoms.

"At the foot of an isolated tree, instead of the little bindweed with its white flower, may sometimes be found the beautifully climbing convolvulus major, of all the lovely colours that can be imagined.

"Sweet peas fasten their tendrils to the bushes, and cover them with the deliciously-scented white, rose-colour, or white and violet butterflies.

"It affords me immense pleasure to fix upon a wild-rose in a hedge, and graft upon it red and white cultivated roses, sometimes single roses of a magnificent golden yellow, then large Provence roses, or others variegated with red and white.

"The rivulets in our neighbourhood do not produce on their banks these forget-me-nots, with their blue flowers, with which the rivulet of my garden is adorned; I mean to save the seed, and scatter it in my walks.

"I have observed two young wild quince trees in the nearest wood; next spring I will engraft upon them two of the best kinds of pears.

"And then, how I enjoy beforehand and in imagination, the pleasure and surprise which the solitary stroller will experience when he meets in his rambles with those beautiful flowers and these delicious fruits!

"This fancy of mine may, one day or another, cause some learned botanist who is herbarizing in these parts a hundred years hence, to print a stupid and startling system. All these beautiful flowers will have become common in the country, and will give it an aspect peculiar to itself; and, perhaps, chance or the wind will cast a few of the seeds or some of them amidst the grass which shall cover my forgotten grave!"

This was the end of the chapter, and then there was a vignette, a very pretty one, of a cross-marked, grass-bound grave.

Some books, generally grown-up ones, put things into your

Juliana Horatia Ewing

head with a sort of rush, and now it suddenly rushed into mine—"*That's what I'll be!* I can think of a name hereafter—but that's what I'll do. I'll take seeds and cuttings, and off-shoots from our garden, and set them in waste places, and hedges, and fields, and I'll make an Earthly Paradise of Mary's Meadow."

CHAPTER VI

The only difficulty about my part was to find a name for it. I might have taken the name of the man who wrote the book—it is Alphonse Karr,—just as Arthur was going to be called John Parkinson. But I am a girl, so it seemed silly to take a man's name. And I wanted some kind of title, too, like King's Apothecary and Herbarist, or Weeding Woman, and Alphonse Karr does not seem to have had any by-name of that sort.

I had put Adela's bonnet on my head to carry it safely, and was still sitting thinking, when the others burst into the library.

Arthur was first, waving a sheet of paper; but when Adela saw the bonnet, she caught hold of his arm and pushed forward.

"Oh, it's sweet! Mary, dear, you're an angel. You couldn't be better if you were a real milliner and lived in Paris. I'm sure you couldn't."

"Mary," said Arthur, "remove that bonnet, which by no means becomes you, and let Adela take it into a corner and gibber over it to herself. I want you to hear this."

"You generally do want the platform," I said, laughing. "Adela, I am very glad you like it. To-morrow, if I can find a bit of pink tissue-paper, I think I could gum on little pleats round the edge of the strings as a finish."

I did not mind how gaudily I dressed the part of Weeding Woman now.

"You are good, Mary. It will make it simply perfect; and, kilts don't you think? Not box pleats?"

Arthur groaned.

"You shall have which you like, dear. Now, Arthur, what is it?"

Arthur shook out his paper, gave it a flap with the back of his hand, as you do with letters when you are acting, and said— "It's to Mother, and when she gets it, she'll be a good deal astonished, I fancy."

When I had heard the letter, I thought so too.

"TO THE QUEEN'S MOST EXCELLENT MAIESTIE—

"MY DEAR MOTHER,—This is to tell you that we have made you Queen of the Blue Robe, and that your son Christopher is a dwarf, and we think you'll both be very much pleased when you hear it. He can do as he likes about having a hump back. When you come home we shall give faire flowers into your Highnesse hands—that is if you'll do what I'm going to ask you, for nobody can grow flowers out of nothing. I want you to write to John—write straight to him, don't put it in your letter to Father—and tell him that you have given us leave to have some of the seedlings out of the frames, and that he's to dig us up a good big clump of daffodils out of the shrubbery—and we'll divide them fairly, for Harry is the Honestest Root-gatherer that ever came over to us. We have turned the whole of our gardens into a *Paradisi in sole Paradisus terrestris*, if you can construe that; but we must have something to make a start. He's got no end of bedding things over—that are doing nothing in the Kitchen Garden and might just as well be in our Earthly Paradise. And please tell him to keep us a tiny pinch of seed at the bottom of every paper when he is sowing the annuals. A little goes a long way, particularly of poppies. And you might give him a hint to let us have a flower-pot or two now and then (I'm sure he takes ours if he finds any of our dead window-plants lying about), and that he needn't be so mighty mean about the good earth in the potting-shed, or the labels either, they're dirt cheap. Mind you write straight. If only you let John know that the gardens don't entirely belong to him, you'll see that what's spare from the big garden would more than set us going; and it shall further encourage him to accomplish the remainder, who in praying that your Highnesse may enjoy the heavenly Paradise after the many years fruition of this earthly,

"Submitteth to be, Your Maiestie's,

"In all humble devotion,

"JOHN PARKINSON,

"King's Apothecary and Herbarist.

"P.S.—It was Mary's idea."

"My *dear* Arthur!" said I.

"Well, I know it's not very well mixed," said Arthur. "Not half so well as I intended at first. I meant to write it all in the Parkinson style. But then, I thought, if I put the part about John in queer language and old spelling, she mightn't understand what we want. But every word of the end comes out of the Dedication; I copied it the other day, and I think she'll find it a puzzlewig when she comes to it."

After which Arthur folded his paper and put it into an envelope which he licked copiously, and closed the letter with a great deal of display. But then his industry coming to an abrupt end, as it often did, he tossed it to me, saying, "You can address it, Mary;" so I enclosed it in my own letter to thank Mother for the book, and I fancy she did write to our gardener, for he gave us a good lot of things, and was much more good-natured than usual.

After Arthur had tossed his letter to me, he clasped his hands over his head and walked up and down thinking. I thought he was calculating what he should be able to get out of John, for when you are planning about a garden, you seem to have to do so much calculating. Suddenly he stopped in front of me and threw down his arms. "Mary," he said, "if Mother were at home, she *would* despise us for selfishness, wouldn't she just?"

"I don't think it's selfish to want spare things for our gardens, if she gives us leave," said I.

"I'm not thinking of that," said Arthur; "and you're not selfish, you never are; but she would despise me, and Adela, and Harry, because we've taken your game, and got our parts, and you've made that preposterous bonnet for Adela to be the Weeding Woman in—much she'll weed!—"

"I *shall* weed," said Adela.

"Oh, yes! You'll weed,—Groundsel!—and leave Mary to get up the docks and dandelions, and clear away the heap. But, never mind. Here we've taken Mary's game, and she hasn't even got a part."

"Yes," said I, "I have; I have got a capital part. I have only to think of a name."

"How shall you be dressed?" asked Adela.

"I don't know yet," said I. "I have only just thought of the part."

"Are you sure it's a good-enough one?" asked Harry, with a grave and remorseful air; "because, if not, you must take Francis le Vean. Girls are called Frances sometimes."

I explained, and I read aloud the bit that had struck my fancy.

Arthur got restless half-way through, and took out the Book of Paradise. His letter was on his mind. But Adela was truly delighted.

"Oh, Mary," she said. "It is lovely. And it just suits you. It suits you much better than being a Queen."

"Much better," said I.

"You'll be exactly the reverse of me," said Harry. "When I'm digging up, you'll be putting in."

"Mary," said Arthur, from the corner where he was sitting with the Book of Paradise in his lap, "what have you put a mark in the place about honeysuckle for?"

"Oh, only because I was just reading there when James brought the letters."

"John Parkinson can't have been quite so nice a man as Alphonse Karr," said Adela; "not so unselfish. He took care of the Queen's Gardens, but he didn't think of making the lanes and hedges nice for poor wayfarers."

I was in the rocking-chair, and I rocked harder to shake up something that was coming into my head. Then I remembered.

"Yes, Adela, he did—a little. He wouldn't root up the honey-suckle out of the hedges (and I suppose he wouldn't let his root-gatherers grub it up, either); he didn't put it in the Queen's Gardens, but left it wild outside—"

"To serve their senses that travel by it, or have no garden," interrupted Arthur, reading from the book, "and, oh, Mary! that reminds me—*travel—travellers.* I've got a name for your part just coming into my head. But it dodges out again like a wire-worm through a three-pronged fork. *Travel—traveler — travellers*—what's the common name for the—oh, dear! the what's his name that scrambles about in the hedges. A flower—you know?"

"Deadly Nightshade?" said Harry.

"Deadly fiddlestick!—"

"Bryony?" I suggested.

"Oh, no; it begins with C."

"Clematis?" said Adela.

"Clematis. Right you are, Adela. And the common name for Clematis is Traveller's Joy. And that's the name for you, Mary, because you're going to serve their senses that travel by hedges and ditches and perhaps have no garden."

"Traveller's Joy," said Harry. "Hooray!"

"Hooray!" said Adela, and she waved the Weeding Woman's bonnet.

It was a charming name, but it was too good for me, and I said so.

Arthur jumped on the rockers, and rocked me to stop my talking. When I was far back, he took the point of my chin in his two hands and lifted up my cheeks to be kissed, saying in his very kindest way, "It's not a bit too good for you—it's you all over."

Then he jumped off as suddenly as he had jumped on, and as I went back with a bounce he cried, "Oh, Mary! give me back that letter. I must put another postscript and another puzzlewig. 'P.P.S.—Excellent Majesty: Mary will still be our Little Mother on all common occasions, as you wished, but in the Earthly Paradise we call her Traveller's Joy.'"

CHAPTER VII

There are two or three reasons why the part of Traveller's Joy suited me very well. In the first place it required a good deal of trouble, and I like taking trouble. Then John was willing to let me do many things he would not have allowed the others to do, because he could trust me to be careful and to mind what he said.

On each side of the long walk in the kitchen garden there are flowers between you and the vegetables, herbaceous borders, with nice big clumps of things that have suckers, and off-shoots and seedlings at their feet.

"The Long Walk's the place to steal from if I wasn't an *honest* Root-gatherer," said Harry.

John had lovely poppies there that summer. When I read about the poppies Alphonse Karr sowed in the wild nooks of his native country, it made me think of John's French poppies, and paeony poppies, and ranunculus poppies, and carnation poppies, some very large, some quite small, some round and neat, some full and ragged like Japanese chrysanthemums, but all of such beautiful shades of red, rose, crimson, pink, pale blush, and white, that if they had but smelt like carnations instead of smelling like laudanum when you have the toothache, they would have been quite perfect.

In one way they are nicer than carnations. They have such lots of seed, and it is so easy to get. I asked John to let me have some of the heads. He could not possibly want them all, for each head has enough in it to sow two or three yards of a border. He said I might have what seeds I liked, if I used scissors, and did not drag things out of the ground by pulling. But I was not to let the young gentlemen go seed gathering. "Boys be so destructive," John said.

After a time, however, I persuaded him to let Harry transplant seedlings of the things that sow themselves and come up in the autumn, if they came up a certain distance from the parent plants. Harry got a lot of things for our Paradise in this way; indeed, he would not have got much otherwise, except wild flowers; and, as he said, "How can I be your Honest Root-gatherer if I mayn't gather anything up by the roots?"

I can't help laughing sometimes to think of the morning when he left off being our Honest Root-gatherer. He did look so funny, and so like Chris.

A day or two before, the Scotch Gardener had brought Saxon to see us, and a new kind of mouldiness that had got into his grape vines to show to John.

He was very cross with Saxon for walking on my garden. (And I am sure I quite forgave him, for I am so fond of him, and he knew no better, poor dear!) But, though he kicked Saxon, the Scotch Gardener was kind to us. He told us that the reason our gardens do not do so well as the big garden, and that my *Jules Margottin* has not such big roses as John's *Jules Margottin* is because we have never renewed the soil.

Arthur and Harry got very much excited about this. They made the Scotch Gardener tell them what good soil ought to

Juliana Horatia Ewing

be made of, and all the rest of the day they talked of nothing but *compost*. Indeed Arthur would come into my room and talk about compost after I had gone to bed.

Father's farming man was always much more good-natured to us than John ever was. He would give us anything we wanted. Warm milk when the cows were milked, or sweet-pea sticks, or bran to stuff the dolls' pillows. I've known him take his hedging-bill, in his dinner-hour, and cut fuel for our beacon-fire, when we were playing at a French Invasion. Nothing could be kinder.

Perhaps we do not tease him so much as we tease John. But when I say that, Arthur says, "Now, Mary, that's just how you explain away things. The real difference between John and Michael is, that Michael is good-natured and John is not. Catch John showing me the duck's nest by the pond, or letting you into the cow-house to kiss the new calf between the eyes—if he were farm man instead of gardener!"

And the night Arthur sat in my room, talking about compost, he said, "I shall get some good stuff out of Michael, I know; and Harry and I see our way to road-scrapings if we can't get sand; and we mean to take precious good care John doesn't have all the old leaves to himself. It's the top-spit that puzzles us, and loam is the most important thing of all."

"What is top-spit?" I asked.

"It's the earth you get when you dig up squares of grass out of a field like the paddock. The new earth that's just underneath. I expect John got a lot when he turfed that new piece by the pond, but I don't believe he'd spare us a flower-pot full to save his life."

"Don't quarrel with John, Arthur. It's no good."

"I won't quarrel with him if he behaves himself," said Arthur, "but we mean to have some top-spit somehow."

"If you aggravate him he'll only complain of us to Father."

"I know," said Arthur hotly, "and beastly mean of him, too, when he knows what Father is about this sort of thing."

"I know it's mean. But what's the good of fighting when you'll only get the worst of it?"

"Why to show that you're in the right, and that you know you are," said Arthur. "Good-night, Mary. We'll have a compost heap of our own this autumn, mark my words."

Next day, in spite of my remonstrances, Arthur and Harry came to open war with John, and loudly and long did they rehearse their grievances, when we were out of Father's hearing.

"Have we ever swept our own walks, except that once, long ago, when the German women came round with threepenny brooms?" asked Arthur, throwing out his right arm, as if he were making a speech. "And think of all the years John has been getting leaf mould for himself out of our copper beech leaves, and now refuses us a barrow-load of loam!"

The next morning but one Harry was late for breakfast, and then it seemed that he was not dressing he had gone out,— very early, one of the servants said. It frightened me, and I went out to look for him.

When I came upon him in our gardens, it was he who was frightened.

"Oh, dear," he exclaimed, "I thought you were John."

Juliana Horatia Ewing

I have often seen Harry dirty—very dirty,—but from the mud on his boots to the marks on his face where he had pushed the hair out of his eyes with earthy fingers, I never saw him quite so grubby before. And if there had been a clean place left in any part of his clothes well away from the ground, that spot must have been soiled by a huge and very dirty sack, under the weight of which his poor little shoulders were bent nearly to his knees.

"What are you doing, Honest Root-gatherer?" I asked; "are you turning yourself into a hump-backed dwarf?"

"I'm not honest, and I'm not a Root-gatherer just now," said Harry, when he had got breath after setting down his load. He spoke shyly and a little surlily, like Chris when he is in mischief.

"Harry, what's that?"

"It's a sack I borrowed from Michael. It won't hurt it, it's had mangel-wurzels in already."

"What have you got in it now? It looks dreadfully heavy."

"It *is* heavy, I can tell you," said Harry, with one more rub of his dirty fingers over his face.

"You look half dead. What is it?"

"It's top-spit;" and Harry began to discharge his load on to the walk.

"Oh, Harry; where did you get it?"

"Out of the paddock. I've been digging up turfs and getting this out, and putting the turfs back, and stamping them down not to show, ever since six o'clock. It *was* hard work; and I was so afraid of John coming. Mary, you won't tell tales?"

"No, Harry. But I don't think you ought to have taken it without Mother's leave."

"I don't think you can call it stealing," said Harry. "Fields are a kind of wild places anyhow, and the paddock belongs to Father, and it certainly doesn't belong to John."

"No," said I, doubtfully.

"I won't get any more; it's dreadfully hard work," said Harry, but as he shook the sack out and folded it up, he added (in rather a satisfied tone), "I've got a good deal."

I helped him to wash himself for breakfast, and half-way through he suddenly smiled and said, "John Parkinson will be glad when he sees *you-know-what*, Mary, whatever the other John thinks of it."

But Harry did not cut any more turfs without leave, for he told me that he had a horrid dream that night of waking up in prison with a warder looking at him through a hole in the door of his cell, and finding out that he was in penal servitude for stealing top-spit from the bottom of the paddock, and Father would not take him out of prison, and that Mother did not know about it.

However, he and Arthur made a lot of compost. They said we couldn't possibly have a Paradise without it.

It made them very impatient. We always want the spring and summer and autumn and winter to get along faster than they do. But this year Arthur and Harry were very impatient with summer.

They were nearly caught one day by Father coming home just as they had got through the gates with Michael's old sack full of road-scrapings, instead of sand (we have not any sand growing near us, and silver sand is rather dear), but we did get leaves together and stacked them to rot into leaf mould.

Leaf mould is splendid stuff, but it takes a long time for the leaves to get mouldy, and it takes a great many too. Arthur is rather impatient, and he used to say—"I never saw leaves stick on to branches in such a way. I mean to get into some of these old trees and give them a good shaking to remind them what time of year it is. If I don't we shan't have anything like enough leaves for our compost."

CHAPTER VIII

Mother was very much surprised by Arthur's letter, but not so much puzzled as he expected. She knew Parkinson's *Paradisus* quite well, and only wrote to me to ask, "What are the boys after with the old books? Does your Father know?"

But when I told her that he had given us leave to be in the library, and that we took great care of the books, and how much we enjoyed the ones about gardening, and all that we were going to do, she was very kind indeed, and promised to put on a blue dress and lace ruffles and be Queen of our Earthly Paradise as soon as she came home.

When she did come home she was much better, and so was Chris. He was delighted to be our Dwarf, but he wanted to have a hump, and he would have such a big one that it would not keep in its place, and kept slipping under his arm and into all sorts of queer positions.

Not one of us enjoyed our new game more than Chris did, and he was always teasing me to tell him the story I had told the others, and to read out the names of the flowers which "the real Queen" had in her "real paradise." He made Mother promise to try to get him a bulb of the real Dwarf Daffodil as his next birthday present, to put in his own garden.

Juliana Horatia Ewing

"And I'll give you some compost," said Arthur. "It'll be ever so much better than a stupid book with 'stuff' in it."

Chris did seem much stronger. He had colour in his cheeks, and his head did not look so large. But he seemed to puzzle over things in it as much as ever, and he was just as odd and quaint.

One warm day I had taken the *Tour round my Garden* and was sitting near the bush in the little wood behind our house, when Chris came after me with a Japanese fan in his hand, and sat down cross-legged at my feet. As I was reading, and Mother has taught us not to interrupt people when they are reading, he said nothing, but there he sat.

"What is it, Chris?" said I.

"I am discontented," said Chris.

"I'm very sorry," said I.

"I don't think I'm selfish, particularly, but I'm discontented."

"What about?"

"Oh, Mary, I do wish I had not been away when you invented Paradise, then I should have had a name in the game."

"You've got a name, Chris. You're the Dwarf."

"Ah, but what was the Dwarf's name?"

"I don't know," I admitted.

"No; that's just it. I've only one name, and Arthur and Harry have two. Arthur is a Pothecary" (Chris could never be induced to accept Apothecary as one word), "and he's John Parkinson as well. Harry is Honest Root-gatherer, and he is Francis le Vean. If I'd not been away I should have had two names."

"You can easily have two names," said I. "We'll call the Dwarf Thomas Brown."

Chris shook his big head.

"No, no. That wasn't his name; I know it wasn't. It's only stuff. I want another name out of the old book."

I dared not tell him that the Dwarf was not in the old book. I said:

"My dear Chris, you really are discontented; we can't all have double names. Adela has only one name, she is Weeding Woman and nothing else; and I have only one name, I'm Traveller's Joy, and that's all."

"But you and Adela are girls," said Chris, complacently: "The boys have two names."

I suppressed some resentment, for Christopher's eyes were beginning to look weary, and said:

"Shall I read to you for a bit?"

"No, don't read. Tell me things out of the old book. Tell me about the Queen's flowers. Don't tell me about daffodils, they make me think what a long way off my birthday is, and I'm quite discontented enough."

And Chris sighed, and lay down on the grass, with one arm

under his head, and his fan in his hand; and, as well as I could remember, I told him all about the different varieties of Cowslips, down to the Franticke, or Foolish Cowslip, and he became quite happy.

Dear Father is rather short-sighted, but he can hold a round glass in his eye without cutting himself. It was the other eye which was next to Chris at prayers the following morning; but he saw his legs, and the servants had hardly got out of the hall before he shouted, "Pull up your stockings, Chris!"—and then to Mother, "Why do you keep that sloven of a girl Bessy, if she can't dress the children decently? But I can't conceive what made you put that child into knickerbockers, he can't keep his stockings up."

"Yes, I can," said Christopher, calmly, looking at his legs.

"Then what have you got 'em down for?" shouted Father.

"They're not all down," said Chris, his head still bent over his knees, till I began to fear he would have a fit.

"One of 'em is, anyhow. I saw it at prayers. Pull it up."

"Two of them are," said Christopher, never lifting his admiring gaze from his stockings. "Two of them are down, and two of them are up, quite up, quite tidy."

Dear Father rubbed his glass and put it back into his eye.

"Why, how many stockings have you got on?"

"Four," said Chris, smiling serenely at his legs; "and it isn't Bessy's fault. I put 'em all on myself, every one of them."

At this minute James brought in the papers, and Father only

laughed, and said, "I never saw such a chap," and began to read. He is very fond of Christopher, and Chris is never afraid of him.

I was going out of the room, and Chris followed me into the hall, and drew my attention to his legs, which were clothed in four stockings; one pair, as he said, being drawn tidily up over his knees, the other pair turned down with some neatness in folds a little above his ankles.

"Mary," he said, "I'm contented now."

"I'm very glad, Chris. But do leave off staring at your legs. All the blood will run into your head."

"I wish things wouldn't always get into *my* head, and nobody else's," said Chris, peevishly, as he raised it; but when he looked back at his stockings, they seemed to comfort him again.

"Mary, I've found another name for myself."

"Dear Chris! I'm so glad."

"It's a real one, out of the old book. I thought of it entirely by myself."

"Good Dwarf. What is your name?"

"*Hose-in-Hose*," said Christopher, still smiling down upon his legs.

CHAPTER IX

Alas for the hose-in-hose!

I laughed over Christopher and his double stockings, and I danced for joy when Bessy's aunt told me that she had got me a fine lot of roots of double cowslips. I never guessed what misery I was about to suffer, because of the hose-in-hose.

I had almost forgotten that Bessy's aunt knew double cowslips. After I became Traveller's Joy I was so busy with wayside planting that I had thought less of my own garden than usual, and had allowed Arthur to do what he liked with it as part of the Earthly Paradise (and he was always changing his plans), but Bessy's aunt had not forgotten about it, which was very good of her.

The Squire's Weeding Woman is old enough to be Bessy's aunt, but she has an aunt of her own, who lives seven miles on the other side of the Moor, and the Weeding Woman does not get to see her very often. It is a very out-of-the-way village, and she has to wait for chances of a cart and team coming and going from one of the farms, and so get a lift.

It was the Weeding Woman's aunt who sent me the hose-in-hose.

The Weeding Woman told me—"Aunt be mortal fond of her flowers, but she've no notions of gardening, not in the ways of a gentleman's garden. But she be after 'em all along, so well as the roomatiz in her back do let her, with an old shovel and a bit of stuff to keep the frost out, one time, and the old shovel and a bit of stuff to keep 'em moistened from the drought, another time; cuddling of 'em like Christians. 'Ee zee, Miss, Aunt be advanced in years; her family be off her mind, zum married, zum buried; and it zim as if her flowers be like new childern for her, spoilt childern, too, as I zay, and most fuss about they that be least worth it, zickly uns and contrairy uns, as parents will. Many's time I do say to she—'Th' Old Zquire's garden, now, 'twould zim strange to thee, sartinly 'twould! How would 'ee feel to see Gardener zowing's spring plants by the hunderd, and a-throwing of 'em away by the score when beds be vull, and turning of un out for bedding plants, and throwing they away when he'eve made his cuttings?' And she 'low she couldn't abear it, no more'n see Herod a mass-sakering of the Innocents. But if 'ee come to Bible, I do say Aunt put me in mind of the par'ble of the talents, she do, for what you give her she make ten of, while other folks be losing what they got. And 'tis well too, for if 'twas not for givin' of un away, seeing's she lose nothing and can't abear to destry nothin', and never takes un up but to set un again, six in place of one, as I say, with such a mossel of a garden, 'Aunt, where would you be?' And she 'low she can't tell, but the Lard would provide. 'Thank He,' I says, 'you be so out o' way, and 'ee back so bad, and past travelling, zo there be no chance of 'ee ever seem' Old Zquire's Gardener's houses and they stove plants;' for if Gardener give un a pot, sure's death her'd set it in the chimbly nook on frosty nights, and put bed-quilt over un, and any cold corner would do for she."

At this point the Weeding Woman became short of breath, and I managed to protest against taking so many plants of

Juliana Horatia Ewing

the hose-in-hose.

"Take un and welcome, my dear, take un and welcome," replied Bessy's aunt. "I did say to Aunt to keep two or dree, but 'One be aal I want,' her says, 'I'll have so many agin in a few years, dividin' of un in autumn,' her says. 'Thee've one foot in grave, Aunt,' says I, 'it don't altogether become 'ee to forecast autumns,' I says, 'when next may be your latter end, 's like as not.' 'Niece,' her says, 'I be no ways presuming. His will be done,' her says, 'but if I'm spared I'll rear un, and if I'm took, 'twill be where I sha'n't want un. Zo let young lady have un,' her says. And there a be!"

When I first saw the nice little plants, I did think of my own garden, but not for long. My next and final thought was— "Mary's Meadow!"

Since I became Traveller's Joy, I had chiefly been busy in the hedge-rows by the high-roads, and in waste places, like the old quarry, and very bare and trampled bits, where there seemed to be no flowers at all.

You cannot say that of Mary's Meadow. Not to be a garden, it is one of the most flowery places I know. I did once begin a list of all that grows in it, but it was in one of Arthur's old exercise-books, which he had "thrown in," in a bargain we had, and there were very few blank pages left. I had thought a couple of pages would be more than enough, so I began with rather full accounts of the flowers, but I used up the book long before I had written out one half of what blossoms in Mary's Meadow.

Wild roses, and white bramble, and hawthorn, and dogwood, with its curious red flowers; and nuts, and maple, and privet, and all sorts of bushes in the hedge, far more than one would think; and ferns, and the stinking iris, which has such splendid berries, in the ditch—the ditch on the lower side where it is damp, and where I meant to sow forget-me-nots, like Alphonse Karr, for there are none there as it happens. On the other side, at the top of the field, it is dry, and blue succory grows, and grows out on the road beyond. The most beautiful blue possible, but so hard to pick. And there are Lent lilies, and lords and ladies, and ground ivy, which smells herby when you find it, trailing about and turning the colour of Mother's "aurora" wool in green winters; and sweet white violets, and blue dog violets, and primroses, of course, and two or three kinds of orchis, and all over the field cowslips, cowslips, cowslips—to please the nightingale.

And I wondered if the nightingale would find out the hose-in-hose, when I had planted six of them in the sunniest, cosiest corner of Mary's Meadow.

For this was what I resolved to do, though I kept my resolve to myself, for which I was afterwards very glad. I did not tell the others because I thought that Arthur might want some of the plants for our Earthly Paradise, and I wanted to put them all in Mary's Meadow. I said to myself, like Bessy's great-aunt, that "if I was spared" I would go next year and divide the roots of the six, and bring some off-sets to our gardens, but I would keep none back now. The nightingale should have them all.

We had been busy in our gardens, and in the roads and bye-lanes, and I had not been in Mary's Meadow for a long time before the afternoon when I put my little trowel, and a bottle of water, and the six hose-in-hose into a basket, and was glad to get off quietly and alone to plant them. The highways and hedges were very dusty, but there it was very green. The nightingale had long been silent, I do not know where he was, but the rooks were not at all silent; they had been holding a parliament at the upper end of the field this morning, and were now all talking at once, and flapping about the tops of the big elms which were turning bright yellow, whilst down below a flight of starlings had taken their place, and sat in the prettiest circles; and groups of hedge-sparrows flew and mimicked them. And in the fields round about the sheep baaed, and the air, which was very sweet, was so quiet that these country noises were the only sounds to be heard, and they could be heard from very far away.

I had found the exact spot I wanted, and had planted four of the hose-in-hose, and watered them from the bottle, and had the fifth in my hand, and the sixth still in the basket, when all these nice noises were drowned by a loud harsh shout which made me start, and sent the flight of starlings into the next field, and made the hedge-sparrows jump into the hedge.

And when I looked up I saw the Old Squire coming towards me, and storming and shaking his fist at me as he came. But with the other hand he held Saxon by the collar, who was struggling to get away from him and to go to me.

I had so entirely forgotten about Father's quarrel with the Squire, that when the sight of the old gentleman in a rage suddenly reminded me, I was greatly stupefied and confused, and really did not at first hear what he said. But when I understood that he was accusing me of digging cowslips out of his field, I said at once (and pretty loud, for he was deaf) that I was not digging up anything, but was planting double cowslips to grow up and spread amongst the common ones.

I suppose it did sound rather unlikely, as the Old Squire knew nothing about our game, but a thing being unlikely is no reason for calling truthful people liars, and that was what the Old Squire called me.

It choked me, and when he said I was shameless, and that he had caught me with the plants upon me, and yelled to me to empty my basket, I threw away the fifth and sixth hose-in-hose as if they had been adders, but I could not speak again. He must have been beside himself with rage, for he called me all sorts of names, and said I was my father's own child, a liar and a thief. Whilst he was talking about sending me to prison (and I thought of Harry's dream, and turned cold with fear), Saxon was tugging to get to me, and at last he got away and came rushing up.

Now I knew that the Old Squire was holding Saxon back because he thought Saxon wanted to worry me as a trespasser, but I don't know whether he let Saxon go at last, because he thought I deserved to be worried, or whether Saxon got away of himself. When his paws were almost on me the Old Squire left off abusing me, and yelled to the dog, who at last, very unwillingly, went back to him, but when he just got to the Squire's feet he stopped, and pawed the ground in the funny way he sometimes does, and looked up at his master as much as to say, "You see it's only play," and then turned round and raced back to me as hard as he could lay legs to ground. This time he reached me, and jumped to lick my face, and I threw my arms round his neck and burst into tears.

When you are crying and kissing at the same time, you cannot hear anything else, so what more the Old Squire said I do not know.

I picked up my basket and trowel at once, and fled homewards as fast as I could go, which was not very fast, so breathless was I with tears and shame and fright.

When I was safe in our grounds I paused and looked back. The Old Squire was still there, shouting and gesticulating,

Juliana Horatia Ewing

and Saxon was at his heels, and over the hedge two cows were looking at him; but the rooks and the starlings were far off in distant trees and fields.

And I sobbed afresh when I remembered that I had been called a liar and a thief, and had lost every one of my hose-in-hose; and this was all that had come of trying to make an Earthly Paradise of Mary's Meadow, and of taking upon myself the name of Traveller's Joy.

CHAPTER X

I told no one. It was bad enough to think of by myself. I could not have talked about it. But every day I expected that the Old Squire would send a letter or a policeman, or come himself, and rage and storm, and tell Father.

He never did; and no one seemed to suspect that anything had gone wrong, except that Mother fidgeted because I looked ill, and would show me to Dr. Solomon. It is a good thing doctors tell you what they think is the matter, and don't ask you what you think, for I could not have told him about the Squire. He said I was below par, and that it was our abominable English climate, and he sent me a bottle of tonic. And when I had taken half the bottle, and had begun to leave off watching for the policeman, I looked quite well again. So I took the rest, not to waste it, and thought myself very lucky. My only fear now was that Bessy's aunt might ask after the hose in-hose. But she never did.

I had one more fright, where I least expected it. It had never occurred to me that Lady Catherine would take an interest in our game, and want to know what we had done, and what we were doing, and what we were going to do, or I should have been far more afraid of her than of Bessy's aunt. For the Weeding Woman has a good deal of delicacy, and often begs pardon for taking liberties; but if Aunt Catherine takes an

Juliana Horatia Ewing

interest, and wants to know, she asks one question after another, and does not think whether you like to answer or not.

She took an interest in our game after one of Christopher's luncheons with her.

She often asks Chris to go there to luncheon, all by himself. Father is not very fond of his going, chiefly, I fancy, because he is so fond of Chris, and misses him. Sometimes, in the middle of luncheon, he looks at Christopher's empty place, and says, "I wonder what those two are talking about over their pudding. They are the queerest pair of friends." If we ask Chris what they have talked about, he wags his head, and looks very well pleased with himself, and says, "Lots of things. I tell her things, and she tells me things." And that is all we can get out of him.

A few weeks afterwards, after I lost the hose-in-hose, Chris went to have luncheon with Aunt Catherine, and he came back rather later than usual.

"You must have been telling each other a good deal to-day, Chris," I said.

"I told her lots," said Chris, complacently. "She didn't tell me nothing, hardly. But I told her lots. My apple fritter got cold whilst I was telling it. She sent it away, and had two hot ones, new, on purpose for me."

"What *did* you tell her?"

"I told her your story; she liked it very much. And I told her Daffodils, and about my birthday; and I told her Cowslips— all of them. Oh, I told her lots. She didn't tell me nothing."

A few days later, Aunt Catherine asked us to tea—all of us—me, Arthur, Adela, Harry, and Chris. And she asked us all about our game. When Harry said, "I dig up, but Mary plants—not in our garden, but in wild places, and woods, and hedges, and fields," Lady Catherine blew her nose very loud, and said, "I should think you don't do much digging and planting in that field your Father went to law about?" and my teeth chattered so with fright that I think Lady Catherine would have heard them if she hadn't been blowing her nose. But, luckily for me, Arthur said, "Oh, we never go near Mary's Meadow now, we're so busy." And then Aunt Catherine asked what made us think of my name, and I repeated most of the bit from Alphonse Karr, for I knew it by heart now; and Arthur repeated what John Parkinson says about the "Honisucle that groweth wilde in every hedge," and how he left it there, "to serue their senses that trauell by it, or haue no garden;" and then he said, "So Mary is called Traveller's Joy, because she plants flowers in the hedges, to serve their senses that travel by them."

"And who serves them that have no garden?" asked Aunt Catherine, sticking her gold glasses over her nose, and looking at us.

"None of us do," said Arthur, after thinking for a minute.

"Humph!" said Aunt Catherine.

Next time Chris was asked to luncheon, I was asked too. Father laughed at me, and teased me, but I went.

I was very much amused by the airs which Chris gave himself at table. He was perfectly well-behaved, but, in his quiet old-fashioned way, he certainly gave himself airs. We have only one man indoors—James; but Aunt Catherine has three—a butler, a footman, and a second footman. The second footman kept near Christopher, who sat opposite Aunt Catherine (she made me sit on one side), and seemed to watch to attend upon him; but if Christopher did want any thing, he always ignored this man, and asked the butler for it, and called him by his name.

After a bit, Aunt Catherine began to talk about the game again.

"Have you got any one to serve them that have no garden, yet?" she asked.

Christopher shook his head, and said "No."

"Humph," said Aunt Catherine; "better take me into the game."

"Could you be of any use?" asked Christopher. "Toast and water, Chambers."

The butler nodded, as majestically as Chris himself, to the second footman, who flew to replenish the silver mug, which had been Lady Catherine's when she was a little girl. When Christopher had drained it (he is a very thirsty boy), he repeated the question:

"Do you think you could be of any use?"

Mr. Chambers, the butler, never seems to hear anything that people say, except when they ask for something to eat or drink; and he does not often hear that, because he watches to see what you want, and gives it of himself, or sends it by the footman. He looks just as if he was having his photograph taken, staring at a point on the wall and thinking of nothing; but when Christopher repeated his question I saw Chambers frown. I believe he thinks Christopher presumes on Lady

Catherine's kindness, and does not approve of it.

It is quite the other way with Aunt Catherine. Just when you would think she must turn angry, and scold Chris for being rude, she only begins to laugh, and shakes like a jelly (she is very stout), and encourages him. She said—

"Take care all that toast and water doesn't get into your head, Chris."

She said that to vex him, because, ever since he heard that he had water on the brain, Chris is very easily affronted about his head. He was affronted now, and began to eat his bread-and-butter pudding in silence, Lady Catherine still shaking and laughing. Then she wiped her eyes, and said—

"Never mind, old man, I'm going to tell you something. Put the sugar and cream on the table, Chambers, and you needn't wait."

The men went out very quietly, and Aunt Catherine went on—

"Where do you think I was yesterday? In the new barracks— a place I set my face against ever since they began to build it, and spoil one of my best peeps from the Rhododendron Walk. I went to see a young cousin of mine, who was fool enough to marry a poor officer, and have a lot of little boys and girls, no handsomer than you, Chris."

"Are they as handsome?" said Chris, who had recovered himself, and was selecting currants from his pudding, and laying them aside for a final *bonne bouche*.

"Humph! Perhaps not. But they eat so much pudding, and wear out so many boots, that they are all too poor to live anywhere except in barracks."

Christopher laid down his spoon, and looked as he always looks when he is hearing a sad story.

"Is barracks like the workhouse, Aunt Catherine?" he asked.

"A good deal like the workhouse," said Aunt Catherine. Then she went on—"I told her Mother I could not begin calling at the barracks. There are some very low streets close by, and my coachman said he couldn't answer for his horses with bugles, and perhaps guns, going off when you least expect them. I told her I would ask them to dinner; and I did, but they were engaged. Well, yesterday I changed my mind, and I told Harness that I meant to go to the barracks, and the horses would have to take me. So we started. When we were going along the upper road, between the high hedges, what do you think I saw?"

Chris had been going on with his pudding again, but he paused to make a guess.

"A large cannon, just going off?"

"No. If I'd seen that, you wouldn't have seen any more of me. I saw masses of wild clematis scrambling everywhere, so that the hedge looked as if somebody had been dressing it up in tufts of feathers."

As she said this, Lady Catherine held out her hand to me across the table very kindly. She has a fat hand, covered with rings, and I put my hand into it.

"And what do you think came into my head?" she asked.

"Toast and water," said Chris, maliciously.

"No, you monkey. I began to think of hedgeflowers, and travellers, and Traveller's Joy."

Aunt Catherine shook my hand here, and dropped it.

"And you thought how nice it was for the poor travellers to have such nice flowers," said Chris, smiling, and wagging his head up and down.

"Nothing of the kind," said Aunt Catherine, brusquely. "I thought what lots of flowers the travellers had already, without Mary planting any more; and I thought not one traveller in a dozen paid much attention to them—begging John Parkinson's pardon—and how much more in want of flowers people 'that have no garden' are; and then I thought of that poor girl in those bare barracks, whose old home was one of the prettiest places, with the loveliest garden, in all Berkshire."

"Was it an Earthly Paradise?" asked Chris.

"It was, indeed. Well, when I thought of her inside those brick walls, looking out on one of those yards they march about in, now they've cut down all the trees, and planted sentry-boxes, I put my best bonnet out of the window, which always spoils the feather, and told Harness to turn his horses' heads, and drive home again."

"What for?" said Chris, as brusquely as Lady Catherine.

"I sent for Hobbs."

"Hobbs the Gardener?" said Chris.

"Hobbs the Gardener; and I told Chambers to give him the basket from the second peg, and then I sent him into the conservatory to fill it. Mary, my dear, I am very particular about my baskets. If ever I lend you my diamonds, and you lose them, I may forgive you—I shall know *that* was an accident; but if I lend you a basket, and you don't return it, don't look me in the face again. I always write my name on them, so there's no excuse. And I don't know a greater piece of impudence—and people are wonderfully impudent now-a-days—than to think that because a thing only cost fourpence, you need not be at the trouble of keeping it clean and dry, and of sending it back."

"Some more toast and water, please," said Chris.

Aunt Catherine helped him, and continued—"Hobbs is a careful man—he has been with me ten years—he doesn't cut flowers recklessly as a rule, but when I saw that basket I said, 'Hobbs, you've been very extravagant.' He looked ashamed of himself, but he said, 'I understood they was for Miss Kitty, m'm. She's been used to nice gardens, m'm.' Hobbs lived with them in Berkshire before he came to me."

"It was very nice of Hobbs," said Chris, emphatically.

"Humph!" said Aunt Catherine, "the flowers were mine."

"Did you ever get to the barracks?" asked Chris, "and what was they like when you did?"

"They were about as unlike Kitty's old home as anything could well be. She has made her rooms pretty enough, but it was easy to see she is hard up for flowers. She's got an old rose-coloured Sevres bowl that was my Grandmother's, and there it was, filled with bramble leaves and Traveller's Joy (which *she* calls Old Man's Beard; Kitty always would differ from her elders!), and a soup-plate full of forget-me-nots. She said two of the children had half-drowned themselves and lost a good straw hat in getting them for her. Just like their mother, as I told her."

"What did she say when you brought out the basket?" asked Chris, disposing of his reserve of currants at one mouthful, and laying down his spoon.

"She said, 'Oh! oh! oh!' till I told her to say something more amusing, and then she said, 'I could cry for joy!' and, 'Tell Hobbs he remembers all my favourites.'"

Christopher here bent his head over his empty plate, and said grace (Chris is very particular about his grace), and then got down from his chair and went up to Lady Catherine, and threw his arms round her as far as they would go, saying, "You are good. And I love you. I should think she thinked you was a fairy godmother."

After they had hugged each other, Aunt Catherine said, "Will you take me into the game, if I serve them that have no garden?"

Chris and I said "Yes" with one voice.

"Then come into the drawing-room," said Aunt Catherine, getting up and giving a hand to each of us. "And Chris shall give me a name."

Chris pondered a long time on this subject, and seemed a good deal disturbed in his mind. Presently he said, "I *won't* be selfish. You shall have it."

"Shall have what, you oddity?"

"I'm not a oddity, and I'm going to give you the name I invented for myself. But you'll have to wear four stockings, two up and two down."

"Then you may keep *that* name to yourself," said Aunt Catherine.

Christopher looked relieved.

"Perhaps you'd not like to be called Old Man's Beard?"

"Certainly not!" said Aunt Catherine.

"It *is* more of a boy's name," said Chris. "You might be the Franticke or Foolish Cowslip, but it is Jack an Apes on Horseback too, and that's a boy's name. You shall be Daffodil, not a dwarf daffodil, but a big one, because you are big. Wait a minute—I know which you shall be. You shall be Nonsuch. It's a very big one, and it means none like it. So you shall be Nonsuch, for there's no one like you."

On which Christopher and Lady Catherine hugged each other afresh.

*　*　*　*　*

"Who told most to-day?" asked Father when we got home.

"Oh, Aunt Catherine. Much most," said Christopher.

CHAPTER XI

The height of our game was in autumn. It is such a good time for digging up, and planting, and dividing, and making cutt-ings, and gathering seeds, and sowing them too. But it went by very quickly, and when the leaves began to fall they fell very quickly, and Arthur never had to go up the trees and shake them.

After the first hard frost we quite gave up playing at the Earthly Paradise; first, because there was nothing we could do, and, secondly, because a lot of snow fell; and Arthur had a grand idea of making-snow statues all along the terrace, so that Mother could see them from the drawing-room windows. We worked very hard, and it was very difficult to manage legs without breaking; so we made most of them Romans in togas, and they looked very well from a distance, and lasted a long time, because the frost lasted.

And, by degrees, I almost forgot that terrible afternoon in Mary's Meadow. Only when Saxon came to see us I told him that I was very glad that no one understood his bark, so that he could not let out what had become of the hose-in-hose.

But when the winter was past, and the snow-drops came out in the shrubbery, and there were catkins on the nut trees, and the missel-thrush we had been feeding in the frost sat out on

Juliana Horatia Ewing

mild days and sang to us, we all of us began to think of our gardens again, and to go poking about "with our noses in the borders," as Arthur said, "as if we were dogs snuffing after truffles." What we really were "snuffing after" were the plants we had planted in autumn, and which were poking and sprouting, and coming up in all directions.

Arthur and Harry did real gardening in the Easter holidays, and they captured Adela now and then, and made her weed. But Christopher's delight was to go with me to the waste places and hedges, where I had planted things as Traveller's Joy, and to get me to show them to him where they had begun to make a Spring start, and to help him to make up rambling stories, which he called "Supposings," of what the flowers would be like, and what this or that traveller would say when he saw them. One of his favourite *supposings* was—"Supposing a very poor man was coming along the road, with his dinner in a handkerchief; and supposing he sat down under the hedge to eat it; and supposing it was cold beef; and he had no mustard; and supposing there was a seed on your nasturtium plants, and he knew it wouldn't poison him; and supposing he ate it with his beef, and it tasted nice and hot, like a pickle, wouldn't he wonder how it got there?"

But when the primroses had been out a long time, and the cowslips were coming into bloom, to my horror Christopher began "supposing" that we should find hose-in-hose in some of the fields, and all my efforts to put this idea out of his head, and to divert him from the search, were utterly in vain.

Whether it had anything to do with his having had water on the brain I do not know, but when once an idea got into Christopher's head there was no dislodging it. He now talked of hose-in-hose constantly. One day he announced that he was "discontented" once more, and should remain so till he had "found a hose-in-hose." I enticed him to a field where I knew it was possible to secure an occasional oxlip, but he only looked pale, shook his head distressingly, and said, "I don't think nothin' of Oxlips." Coloured primroses would not comfort him. He professed to disbelieve in the time-honoured prescription, "Plant a primrose upside down, and it will come up a polyanthus," and refused to help me to make the experiment. At last the worst came. He suddenly spoke, with smiles—"I *know* where we'll find hose-in-hose! In Mary's Meadow. It's the fullest field of cowslips there is. Hurrah! Supposing we find hose-in-hose, and supposing we find green cowslips, and supposing we find curled cowslips or galligaskins, and supposing—"

But I could not bear it, I fairly ran away from him, and shut myself up in my room and cried. I knew it was silly, and yet I could not bear the thought of having to satisfy everybody's curiosity, and describe that scene in Mary's Meadow, which had wounded me so bitterly, and explain why I had not told of it before.

I cried, too, for another reason. Mary's Meadow had been dear to us all, ever since I could remember. It was always our favourite field. We had coaxed our nurses there, when we could induce them to leave the high-road, or when, luckily for us, on account of an epidemic, or for some reason or another, they were forbidden to go gossiping into the town. We had "pretended" fairies in the nooks of the delightfully neglected hedges, and we had found fairy-rings to prove our pretendings true. We went there for flowers; we went there for mushrooms and puff-balls; we went there to hear the nightingale. What cowslip balls and what cowslip tea-parties it had afforded us! It is fair to the Old Squire to say that we were sad trespassers, before he and Father quarrelled and went to law. For Mary's Meadow was a field with every quality to recommend it to childish affections.

Juliana Horatia Ewing

And now I was banished from it, not only by the quarrel, of which we had really not heard much, or realized it as fully, but by my own bitter memories. I cried afresh to think I should never go again to the corner where I always found the earliest violets; and then I cried to think that the nightingale would soon be back, and how that very morning, when I opened my window, I had heard the cuckoo, and could tell that he was calling from just about Mary's Meadow.

I cried my eyes into such a state, that I was obliged to turn my attention to making them fit to be seen; and I had spent quite half-an-hour in bathing them and breathing on my handkerchief, and dabbing them, which is more soothing, when I heard Mother calling me. I winked hard, drew a few long breaths, rubbed my cheeks, which were so white they showed up my red eyes, and ran down-stairs. Mother was coming to meet me. She said—"Where is Christopher?"

It startled me. I said, "He was with me in the garden, about— oh, about an hour ago; have you lost him? I'll go and look for him."

And I snatched up a garden hat, which shaded my swollen eyelids, and ran out. I could not find him anywhere, and becoming frightened, I ran down the drive, calling him as I went, and through the gate, and out into the road.

A few yards farther on I met him.

That child is most extraordinary. One minute he looks like a ghost; an hour later his face is beaming with a radiance that seems absolutely to fatten him under your eyes. That was how he looked just then as he came towards me, smiling in an effulgent sort of way, as if he were the noonday sun—no less, and carrying a small nosegay in his hand.

When he came within hearing he boasted, as if he had been Caesar himself—

"I went; I found it. I've got them."

And as he held his hand up, and waved the nosegay—I knew all. He had been to Mary's Meadow, and the flowers between his fingers were hose-in-hose.

Juliana Horatia Ewing

CHAPTER XII

"I won't be selfish, Mary," Christopher said. "You invented the game, and you told me about them. You shall have them in water on your dressing-table; they might get lost in the nursery. Bessy is always throwing things out. To-morrow I shall go and look for galligaskins."

I was too glad to keep them from Bessy's observation, as well as her unparalleled powers of destruction, which I knew well. I put them into a slim glass on my table, and looked stupidly at them, and then out of the window at Mary's Meadow.

So they had lived—and grown—and settled there—and were now in bloom. *My* plants.

Next morning I was sitting, drawing, in the school-room window, when I saw the Old Squire coming up the drive. There is no mistaking him when you can see him at all. He is a big, handsome old man, with white whiskers, and a white hat, and white gaiters, and he generally wears a light coat, and a flower in his button-hole. The flower he wore this morning looked like—, but I was angry with myself for thinking of it, and went on drawing again, as well as I could, for I could not help wondering why he was coming to our house. Then it struck me he might have seen Chris trespassing, and he might be coming at last to lay a formal complaint.

Twenty minutes later James came to tell me that Father wished to see me in the library, and when I got there, Father was just settling his eye-glass in his eye, and the Old Squire was standing on the hearth-rug, with a big piece of paper in his hand. And then I saw that I was right, and that the flowers in his button-hole were hose-in-hose.

As I came in he laid down the paper, took the hose-in-hose out of his button-hole in his left hand, and held out his right hand to me, saying: "I'm more accustomed to public speaking than to private speaking, Miss Mary. But—will you be friends with me?"

In Mary's Meadow my head had got all confused, because I was frightened. I was not frightened to-day, and I saw the whole matter in a moment. He had found the double cowslips, and he knew now that I was neither a liar nor a thief. I was glad, but I could not feel very friendly to him. I said, "You can speak when you are angry."

Though he was behind me, I could feel Father coming nearer, and I knew somehow that he had taken out his glass again to rub it and put it back, as he does when he is rather surprised or amused. I was afraid he meant to laugh at me afterwards, and he can tease terribly, but I could not have helped saying what came into my head that morning if I had tried. When you have suffered a great deal about anything, you cannot sham, not even politeness.

The Old Squire got rather red. Then he said, "I am afraid I am very hasty, my dear, and say very unjustifiable things. But I am very sorry, and I beg your pardon. Will you forgive me?"

I said, "Of course, if you're sorry, I forgive you, but you have been a very long time in repenting."

Which was true. If I had been cross with one, of the others, and had borne malice for five months, I should have thought myself very wicked. But when I had said it, I felt sorry, for the old gentleman made no answer. Father did not speak either, and I began to feel very miserable. I touched the flowers, and the Old Squire gave them to me in silence. I thanked him very much, and then I said—

"I am very glad you know about it now.... I'm very glad they lived ... I hope you like them?... I hope, if you do like them, that they'll grow and spread all over your field."

The Old Squire spoke at last. He said, "It is not my field any longer."

I said, "Oh, why?"

"I have given it away; I have been a long time in repenting, but when I did repent I punished myself. I have given it away."

It overwhelmed me, and when he took up the big paper again, I thought he was going, and I tried to stop him, for I was sorry I had spoken unkindly to him, and I wanted to be friends.

"Please don't go," I said. "Please stop and be friends. And oh, please, please don't give Mary's Meadow away. You mustn't punish yourself. There's nothing to punish yourself for. I forgive you with all my heart, and I'm sorry I spoke crossly. I have been so very miserable, and I was so vexed at wasting the hose-in-hose, because Bessy's great-aunt gave them to me, and I've none left. Oh, the unkindest thing you could do to me now would be to give away Mary's Meadow."

The Old Squire had taken both my hands in his, and now he asked very kindly—"Why, my dear, why don't you want me to give away Mary's Meadow?"

"Because we are so fond of it. And because I was beginning to hope that now we're friends, and you know we don't want to steal your things, or to hurt your field, perhaps you would let us play in it sometimes, and perhaps have Saxon to play with us there. We are so very fond of him too."

"You are fond of Mary's Meadow?" said the Old Squire.

"Yes, yes! We have been fond of it all our lives. We don't think there is any field like it, and I don't believe there can be. Don't give it away. You'll never get one with such flowers in it again. And now there are hose-in-hose, and they are not at all common. Bessy's aunt's aunt has only got one left, and she's taking care of it with a shovel. And if you'll let us in we'll plant a lot of things, and do no harm, we will indeed. And the nightingale will be here directly. Oh, don't give it away!"

My head was whirling now with the difficulty of persuading him, and I did not hear what he said across me to my father. But I heard Father's reply—"Tell her yourself, sir."

On which the Old Squire stuffed the big paper into my arms, and put his hand on my head and patted it.

"I told you I was a bad hand at talking, my dear," he said, "but Mary's Meadow is given away, and that's the Deed of Gift which you've got in your arms, drawn up as tight as any rascal of a lawyer can do it, and that's not so tight, I believe, but what some other rascal of a lawyer could undo it.

Juliana Horatia Ewing

However, they may let you alone. For I've given it to you, my dear, and it is yours. So you can plant, and play, and do what you please there. 'You, and your heirs and assigns, for ever,' as the rascals say."

It was my turn now to be speechless. But as I stared blankly in front of me, I saw that Father had come round, and was looking at me through his eye-glass. He nodded to me, and said, "Yes, Mary, the Squire has given Mary's Meadow to you, and it is yours."

*   *   *   *   *

Nothing would induce the Old Squire to take it back, so I had to have it, for my very own. He said he had always been sorry he had spoken so roughly to me, but he could not say so, as he and Father were not on speaking terms. Just lately he was dining with Lady Catherine, to meet her cousins from the barracks, and she was telling people after dinner about our game (rather mean of her, I think, to let out our secrets at a dinner-party), and when he heard about my planting things in the hedges, he remembered what I had said. And next day he went to the place to look, and there were the hose-in-hose.

Oh, how delighted the others were when they heard that Mary's Meadow belonged to me.

"It's like having an Earthly Paradise given to you, straight off!" said Harry.

"And one that doesn't want weeding," said Adela.

"And oh, Mary, Mary!" cried Arthur. "Think of the yards and yards of top-spit. It does rejoice me to think I can go to you now when I'm making compost, and need not be beholden to that old sell-up-your-grandfather John for as much as would fill Adela's weeding basket, and that's about as small an article as any one can make-believe with."

"It's very heavy when it's full," said Adela.

"Is everything hers?" asked Christopher. "Is the grass hers, and the trees hers, and the hedges hers, and the rooks hers, and the starling hers, and will the nightingale be hers when he comes home, and if she could dig through to the other side of the world, would there be a field the same size in Australia that would be hers, and are the sheep hers, and—"

"For mercy's sake stop that catalogue, Chris," said Father. "Of course the sheep are not hers; they were moved yesterday. By the bye, Mary, I don't know what you propose to do with your property, but if you like to let it to me, I'll turn some sheep in to-morrow, and I'll pay you so much a year, which I advise you to put into the Post Office Savings Bank."

I couldn't fancy Mary's Meadow always without sheep, so I was too thankful; though at first I could not see that it was fair that dear Father should let me have his sheep to look pretty in my field for nothing, and pay me, too. He is always teasing me about my field, and he teases me a good deal about the Squire, too. He says we have set up another queer friendship in the family, and that the Old Squire and I are as odd a pair as Aunt Catherine and Chris.

I am very fond of the Old Squire now, and he is very kind to me. He wants to give me Saxon, but I will not accept him. It would be selfish. But the Old Squire says I had better take him, for we have quite spoilt him for a yard dog by petting him, till he has not a bit of savageness left in him. We do not believe Saxon ever was savage; but I daren't say so to the Old Squire, for he does not like you to think you know better than he does about anything. There is one other subject on which he expects to be humoured, and I am careful not to offend him. He cannot tolerate the idea that he might be supposed to have yielded to Father the point about which they went to law, in giving Mary's Meadow to me. He is always lecturing me on encroachments, and the abuse of privileges, and warning me to be very strict about trespassers on the path through Mary's Meadow; and now that the field is mine, nothing will induce him to walk in it without asking my leave. That is his protest against the decision from which he meant to appeal.

Though I have not accepted Saxon, he spends most of his time with us. He likes to come for the night, because he sleeps on the floor of my room, instead of in a kennel, which must be horrid, I am sure. Yesterday, the Old Squire said, "One of these fine days, when Master Saxon does not come home till morning, he'll find a big mastiff in his kennel, and will have to seek a home for himself where he can."

Chris has been rather whimsical lately. Father says Lady Catherine spoils him. One day he came to me, looking very peevish, and said, "Mary, if a hedgehog should come and live in one of your hedges, Michael says he would be yours, he's sure. If Michael finds him, will you give him to me?"

"Yes, Chris; but what do you want with a hedgehog?"

"I want him to sleep by my bed," said Chris. "You have Saxon by your bed; I want something by mine. I want a hedgehog. I feel discontented without a hedgehog. I think I might have something the matter with my brain if I didn't get a hedgehog pretty soon. Can I go with Michael and look for him this afternoon?" and he put his hand to his forehead.

"Chris, Chris!" I said, "you should not be so sly. You're a

real slyboots. Double-stockings and slyboots." And I took him on my lap.

Chris put his arms round my neck, and buried his cheek against mine.

"I won't be sly, Mary," he whispered; and then, hugging me as he hugs Lady Catherine, he added, "For I do love you; for you are a darling, and I do really think it always was yours."

"What, Chris?"

"If not," said Chris, "why was it always called MARY'S MEADOW?"

Juliana Horatia Ewing

LETTERS FROM A LITTLE GARDEN

LETTER I

"All is fine that is fit."

—*Old Proverb*

DEAR LITTLE FRIEND,

When, with the touching confidence of youth, that your elders have made-up as well as grown-up minds on all subjects, you asked my opinion on *Ribbon-gardening*, the above proverb came into my head, to the relief of its natural tendency to see an inconvenient number of sides to every question. The more I reflect upon it, the more I am convinced it is a comfortably compact confession of my faith on all matters decorative, and thence on the decoration of gardens.

I take some credit to myself for having the courage of my moderation, since you obviously expect a more sweeping reply. The bedding-out system is in bad odour just now; and you ask, "Wasn't it hideous?" and "Wasn't it hateful?" and "Will it ever come into fashion again, to the re-extermination of the dear old-fashioned flowers which we are now slowly, and with pains, recalling from banishment?"

To discover one's own deliberate opinion upon a subject is not always easy—prophetic opinions one must refuse to offer. But I feel no doubt whatever that the good lady who shall coddle this little garden at some distant date after me will be quite as fond of her borders as I am of mine; and I suspect that these will be about as like each other as our respective best bonnets.

The annals of Fashion must always be full of funny stories. I know two of the best amateur gardeners of the day; they are father and son. The father, living *and gardening* still (he sent me a specimen lily lately by parcel post, and is beholden to no one for help, either with packing or addressing, in his constant use of this new convenience), is making good way between ninety and a hundred years of age. What we call old-fashioned flowers were the pets of his youth. About the time when ribbon-bordering "came in," he changed his residence, and, in the garden where he had cultivated countless kinds of perennials, his son reigned in his stead. The horticultural taste proved hereditary, but in the younger man it took the impress of the fashion of his day. Away went the "herbaceous stuff" on to rubbish heaps, and the borders were soon gay with geraniums, and kaleidoscopic with calceolarias. But "the whirligig of Time brings in his revenges," and, perhaps, a real love for flowers could never, in the nature of things, have been finally satisfied by the dozen or by the score; so it came to pass that the garden is once more herbaceous, and far-famed as such. The father—a *perennial* gardener in more senses than one, long may he flourish!—has told me, chuckling, of many a penitential pilgrimage to the rubbish heaps, if haply fragments could be found of the herbaceous treasures which had been so rashly cast away.

Juliana Horatia Ewing

Doubtless there were many restorations. Abandoned "bedding stuff" soon perishes, but uprooted clumps of "herbaceous stuff" linger long in shady corners, and will sometimes flower pathetically on the heap where they have been thrown to rot.

I once saw a fine Queen Anne country house—an old one; not a modern imitation. Chippendale had made the furniture. He had worked in the house. Whether the chairs and tables were beautiful or not is a matter of taste, but they were well made and seasoned; so, like the herbaceous stuff, they were hardy. The next generation decided that they were ugly. New chairs and tables were bought, and the Chippendale "stuff" was sent up into the maids' bedrooms, and down to the men's. It drifted into the farmhouses and cottages on the estate. No doubt a good deal was destroyed. The caprices of fashion are not confined to one class, and the lower classes are the more prodigal and destructive. I have seen the remains of Elizabethan bedsteads under hay-ricks, and untold "old oak" has fed the cottage fire. I once asked a village maiden why the people made firewood of carved arm-chairs, when painted pinewood, upholstered in American cloth, is, if lovelier, not so lasting. Her reply was—"They get stalled on[3] 'em." And she added: "Maybe a man 'll look at an old arm-chair that's stood on t' hearth-place as long as he can remember, and he'll say—I'm fair sick o' t' seet o' *yon*. We mun have a new 'un for t' Feast. *I'll chop thee oop!*"

[Footnote 3: "Stalled on" = tired of. "T' feast" = the village feast, an annual festival and fair, for which most houses in that district are cleaned within and whitewashed without.]

Possibly some of the Chippendale chairs also fell to the hatchet and fed the flames, but most of them bore neglect as well as hardy perennials, and when Queen Anne houses and "old Chips" came into fashion again, there was routing and rummaging from attic to cellar, in farmhouse and cottage, and the banished furniture went triumphantly back to its own place.

I first saw single dahlias in some "little gardens" in Cheshire, five or six years ago. No others had ever been cultivated there. In these quiet nooks the double dahlia was still a new-fangled flower. If the single dahlias yet hold their own, those little gardens must now find themselves in the height of the floral fashion, with the unusual luck of the conservative old woman who "wore her bonnet till the fashions came round again."

It is such little gardens which have kept for us the Blue Primrose, the highly fragrant Summer Roses (including Rose de Meaux, and the red and copper Briar), countless beautiful varieties of Daffy-down-dillies, and all the host of sweet, various and hardy flowers which are now returning, like the Chippendale chairs, from the village to the hall.

It is still in cottage gardens chiefly that the Crown Imperial hangs its royal head. One may buy small sheaves of it in the Taunton market-place on early summer Saturdays. What a stately flower it is! and, in the paler variety, of what an exquisite yellow! I always fancy *Fritillaria Imperialis flava* to be dressed in silk from the Flowery Land—that robe of imperial yellow which only General Gordon and the blood royal of China are entitled to wear!

"All is fine that is fit." And is the "bedding-out" system—Ribbon-gardening—ever fit, and therefore ever fine? My little friend, I am inclined to think that it sometimes is. For long straight borders in parks and public promenades, for some terrace garden on a large scale, viewed perhaps from windows at a considerable distance, and, in a general way, for pleasure-grounds ordered by professional skill, and not by an *amateur* gardener (which, mark you, being interpreted, is gardener *for love*!), the bedding-out style *is* good for general effect, and I think it is capable of prettier ingenuities than one often sees employed in its use. I think that, if I ever gardened in this expensive and mechanical style, I should make "arrangements," a la Whistler, with flowers of various shades of the same colour. But harmony and gradation of colour always give me more pleasure than contrast.

Then, besides the fitness of the gardening to the garden, there is the fitness of the garden to its owner; and the owner must be considered from two points of view, his taste, and his means. Indeed, I think it would be fair to add a third, his leisure.

Now, there are owners of big gardens and little gardens, who like to have a garden (what Englishman does not?), and like to see it gay and tidy, but who don't know one flower from the rest. On the other hand, some scientists are acquainted with botany and learned in horticulture. They know every plant and its value, but they care little about tidiness. Cut flowers are feminine frivolities in their eyes, and they count nosegays as childish gauds, like daisy chains and cowslip balls. They are not curious in colours, and do not know which flowers are fragrant and which are scentless. For them every garden is a botanical garden. Then, many persons fully appreciate the beauty and the scent of flowers, and enjoy selecting and arranging them for a room, who can't abide to handle a fork or meddle with mother earth. Others again, amongst whom I number myself, love not only the lore of flowers, and the sight of them, and the fragrance of them, and the growing of them, and the picking of them, and the arranging of them, but also inherit from Father Adam a natural relish for tilling the ground from whence they were taken and to which they shall return.

With little persons in little gardens, having also little strength and little leisure, this husbandry may not exceed the small uses of fork and trowel, but the earth-love is there, all the same. I remember once, coming among some family papers upon an old letter from my grandmother to my grandfather. She was a clever girl (she did not outlive youth), and the letter was natural and full of energy and point. My grandfather seems to have apologized to his bride for the disorderly state of the garden to which she was about to-go home, and in reply she quaintly and vehemently congratulates herself upon this unpromising fact. For—"I do so dearly love *grubbing.*" This touches another point. She was a botanist, and painted a little. So were most of the lady gardeners of her youth. The education of women was, as a rule, poor enough in those days; but a study of "the Linnean system" was among the elegant accomplishments held to "become a young woman"; and one may feel pretty sure that even a smattering of botanical knowledge, and the observation needed for third or fourth-rate flower-painting, would tend to a love of variety in beds and borders which Ribbon-gardening would by no means satisfy. *Lobelia erinus speciosa* does make a wonderfully smooth blue stripe in sufficient quantities, but that would not console any one who knew or had painted *Lobelia cardinalis*, and *fulgens*, for the banishment of these from the garden.

I think we may dismiss Ribbon-gardening as unfit for a botanist, or for any one who happens to like *grubbing*, or tending his flowers.

Is it ever "fit" in a little garden?

Well, if the owner has either no taste for gardening, or no time, it may be the shortest and brightest plan to get some nurseryman near to fill the little beds and borders with Spring bedding plants for Spring (and let me note that this

Spring bedding, which is of later date than the first rage for ribbon-borders, had to draw its supplies very largely from "herbaceous stuff," *myosotis, viola, aubretia, iberis*, &c., and may have paved the way for the return of hardy perennials into favour), and with Tom Thumb Geranium, Blue Lobelia, and Yellow Calceolaria for the summer and autumn. These latter are most charming plants. They are very gay and persistent whilst they last, and it is not their fault that they cannot stand our winters. They are no invalids till frost comes. With my personal predilections, I like even "bedding stuff" best in variety. The varieties of what we call geraniums are many and most beautiful. I should always prefer a group of individual specimens to a band of one. And never have I seen the canary yellow of calceolarias to such advantage as in an "old-fashioned" rectory-garden in Yorkshire, where they were cunningly used as points of brilliancy at corners of beds mostly filled with "hardy herbaceous stuff."

But there, again, one begins to spend time and taste! Let us admit that, if a little garden must be made gay by the neighbouring nurseryman, it will look very bright, on the "ribbon" system, at a minimum cost of time and trouble—*but not of money!*

Even for a little garden, bedding plants are very expensive. For you must either use plenty, or leave it alone. A ragged ribbon-border can have no admirers.

If time and money are both lacking, and horticulture is not a hobby, divide what sum you are prepared to spend on your little garden in two. Lay out half in making good soil, and spend the rest on a limited range of hardy plants. If mother earth is well fed, and if you have got her *deep down*, and not a surface layer of half a foot on a substratum of builder's rubbish, she will take care of every plant you commit to her hold. I should give up the back of the borders (if the aspect is east or south) to a few very good "perpetual" roses to cut from; dwarfs, not standards; and for the line of colour in front it will be no great trouble to arrange roughly to have red, white, blue, and yellow alternately.

One of the best cheap bedders is Pink Catchfly (*Silene pendula*). Its rosy cushions are as neat and as lasting as Blue Lobelia. It is a hardy annual, but the plants should be autumn sown of the year before. It flowers early and long, and its place might be taken for the autumn by scarlet dwarf nasturtiums, or clumps of geranium. Pink Catchfly, Blue Forget-me-not, White Arabis, and Yellow Viola would make gay any Spring border. Then to show, to last, and to cut from, few flowers rival the self-coloured pansies (Viola class). Blue, white, purple, and yellow alternately, they are charming, and if in good soil, well watered in drought, and constantly cut from, they bloom the whole summer long. And some of them are very fragrant. The secret of success with these is never to leave a flower to go to seed. They are not cut off by autumnal frosts. On the contrary, you can take them up, and divide, and reset, and send a portion to other little gardens where they are lacking.

All mine (and they have been very gay this year and very sweet) I owe to the bounty of friends who garden *non sibi sed toti*.

Lastly, if there is even a very little taste and time to spare, surely nothing can be so satisfactory as a garden full of such flowers as (in the words of John Parkinson) "our English ayre will permitt to be noursed up." Bearing in mind these counsels:

Make a wise selection of hardy plants. Grow only good sorts, and of these choose what suit your soil and climate. Give

Juliana Horatia Ewing

them space and good feeding. Disturb the roots as little as possible, and cut the flowers constantly. Then they will be fine as well as fit.

Good-bye, Little Friend,

Yours, &c.

LETTER II

"The tropics may have their delights; but they have not turf, and the world without turf is a dreary desert. The original Garden of Eden could not have had such turf as one sees in England.

* * * * *

"Woman always did, from the first, make a muss in a garden.

* * * * *

"Nevertheless, what a man needs in gardening is a cast-iron back, with a hinge in it."

Pusley; or, My Summer in a Garden.

—C. D. WARNER

DEAR LITTLE FRIEND,

Do you know the little book from which these sayings are quoted? It is one you can laugh over by yourself, again and again. A very good specimen of that curious, new-world kind of wit—American humour; and also full of the truest sense of natural beauty and of gardening delights.

Mr. Warner is not complimentary to woman's work in the garden, though he displays all the graceful deference of his countrymen to the weaker sex. In the charming dedication to his wife, whilst desiring "to acknowledge an influence which has lent half the charm to my labour," he adds: "If I were in a court of justice, or injustice, under oath, I should not like to say that, either in the wooing days of spring, or under the suns of the summer solstice, you had been, either with hoe, rake, or miniature spade, of the least use in the garden." Perhaps our fair cousins on the other side of the Atlantic do not *grub* so energetically as we do. Certainly, with us it is very common for the ladies of the family to be the practical gardeners, the master of the house caring chiefly for a good general effect, with tidy walks and grassplots, and displaying less of that almost maternal solicitude which does bring flowers to perfection.

I have sometimes thought that it would be a good division of labour in a Little Garden, if, where Joan coddles the roses and rears the seedlings, Darby would devote some of his leisure to the walks and grassplots.

Few things in one's garden are pleasanter to one's own eye, or gain more admiration from others, than well-kept turf. Green grass is one of the charms of the British Isles, which are emerald isles throughout, though Ireland is so *par excellence*. It is so much a matter of course to us that we hardly realize this till we hear or read what foreigners say about it, and also our own American and colonial cousins. We go abroad and revel in real sunshine, and come home with glowing memories to abuse our own cloudy skies; but they come from burnt-up landscapes to refresh their eyes with our perpetual green.

Even a little grassplot well repays pains and care. If you have to make it, never use cheap seed. Buy the very best from seedsmen of repute, or you will get a conglomeration of weeds instead of a greensward of fine grasses and white clover. Trench the ground to an *even* depth, tread it firm, and have light, finely-sifted soil uppermost. Sow thickly early in April, cover lightly, and protect from birds. If the soil is good, and the seed first-rate, your sward will be green the first season.

Turfs make a lawn somewhat quicker than seed. The best are cut from the road-side, but it is a hateful despoiling of one of the fairest of travellers' joys. Those who commit this highway robbery should reckon themselves in honour bound to sow the bare places they leave behind. Some people cut the pieces eighteen inches square, some about a yard long and twelve inches wide. Cut thin, roll up like thin bread-and-butter. When they are laid down, fit close together, like bits of a puzzle, and roll well after laying. If they gape with shrinking, fill in between with finely-sifted soil, and roll again and again.

Strictly speaking, a grassplot should be all grass, grass and a little white clover. "Soldiers" (of the plantain type) are not to be tolerated on a lawn, but I have a weak corner for dog-daisies. I once owned a little garden in Canada, but never a dog-daisy grew there. A lady I knew had one—in a pot—sent from "Home." But even if you have a sentimental fondness for "the pretty things" (as their botanical name signifies), and like to see their little white faces peeping out of the grass, this must not be carried too far. In some soils dog-daisies will soon devour the whole lawn.

How are they, and "soldiers," and other weeds to be extirpated? There are many nostrums, but none so effectual as a patient digging up (with a long "daisy fork") of plant after plant *by the roots*. The whole family party and any chance visitors will not be too many for the work, and, if each labourer is provided with a cast-iron back with a hinge in it, so much the better. A writer in the *Garden* seems to have been very successful with salt, used early in the season and with great care. He says: "After the first cutting in the spring put as much salt on each weed, through the palm of the hand, as will distinctly cover it. In two or three days, depending on the weather, they will turn brown. Those weeds that have escaped can be distinctly seen, and the operation should be repeated. The weeds thus treated die, and in about three weeks the grass will have grown, and there will not be a vestige of disturbance left. Two years ago I converted a rough pasture into a tennis-ground for six courts. Naturally the turf was a mass of rough weeds. It took three days to salt them, and the result was curiously successful."

Another prescription is to cut off the crowns of the offending plants, and dose them with a few drops of carbolic acid.

Grass will only grow dense by constant cutting and moisture. The scythe works best when the grass is wet, and the machine when it is dry. Sweep it and roll it during the winter. Pick off stones, sticks, or anything that "has no business" on it, as you would pick "bits" off a carpet.

If grass grows rank and coarse, a dressing of sand will improve it; if it is poor and easily burned up, give it a sprinkling of soot, or guano, or wood ashes (or all three mixed) before rain. "Slops" are as welcome to parched grass as to half-starved flowers. If the weather is hot and the soil light, it is well occasionally to leave the short clippings of one mowing upon the lawn to protect the roots.

I do not know if it becomes unmanageable, but, in

moderation, I think camomile a very charming intruder on a lawn, and the aromatic scent which it yields to one's tread to be very grateful in the open air. It is pleasant, too, to have a knoll or a bank somewhere, where thyme can grow among the grass. But the subject of flowers that grow well through grass is a large one. It is one also on which the members of our Parkinson Society would do kindly to give us any exceptional experiences, especially in reference to flowers which not only flourish among grass, but do not resent being mown down. The lovely blue windflower (*Anemone Apennina*) is, I believe, one of these.

There is no doubt that now and then plants prefer to meet with a little resistance, and despise a bed that is made too comfortable. Self-sown ones often come up much more vigorously through the hard path than when the seed has fallen within the border. The way to grow the parsley fern is said to be to clap a good big stone on his crown very early in the spring, and let him struggle out at all corners from underneath it. It is undoubtedly a comfort to rock-plants and creeping things to be planted with a stone over their feet to keep them cool!

Which reminds me of stones for bordering. I think they make the best of all edgings for a Little Garden. Box-edgings are the prettiest, but they are expensive, require good keeping, and harbour slugs. For that matter, most things seem to harbour slugs in any but a very dry climate, and there are even more prescriptions for their destruction than that of lawn weeds. I don't think lime does much, nor soot. Wet soon slakes them. Thick slices of turnip are attractive. Slugs really do seem to like them, even better than one's favourite seedlings. Little heaps of bran also, and young lettuces. My slugs do not care for cabbage leaves, and they are very untidy. Put thick slices of turnip near your auriculas, favourite primroses and polyanthuses, and Christmas roses, and near anything tender and not well established, and overhaul them early in the morning. "You can't get up too early, if you have a garden," says Mr. Warner; and he adds: "Things appear to go on in the night in the garden uncommonly. It would be less trouble to stay up than it is to get up so early!"

To return to stone edgings. When quite newly laid, like miniature rockwork, they are, perhaps, the least bit cockneyfied, and suggestive of something between oyster-shell borderings and mock ruins. But this effect very rapidly disappears as they bury themselves in cushions of pink catch-fly (v. *compacta*), or low-growing pinks, tiny camp-anulas, yellow viola, London pride, and the vast variety of rock-plants, "alpines," and low-growing "herbaceous stuff," which delight in squeezing up to a big cool stone that will keep a little moisture for their rootlets in hot summer weather. This is a much more interesting kind of edging than any one kind of plant can make, I think, and in a Little Garden it is like an additional border, leaving the other free for bigger plants. If one kind is preferred, for a light soil there is nothing like thrift. And the white thrift is very silvery and more beautiful than the pink. There is a large thrift, too, which is handsome. But I prefer stones, and I like varieties of colour—bits of grey boulder, and red and yellow sandstone.

I like warm colour also on the walks. I should always have red walks if I could afford them. There is a red material, the result of some process of burning, which we used to get in the iron and coal districts of Yorkshire, which I used to think very pretty, but I do not know what it is called.

Good walks are a great luxury. It is a wise economy to go round your walks after rain and look for little puddles; make a note of where the water lodges and fill it up. Keep gratings swept. If the grating is free and there is an overflow not to be accounted for, it is very possible that a drain-pipe some-where is choke-full of the roots of some tree.

Some people advise hacking up your walks from time to time, and other people advise you not. Some people say there is nothing like salt to destroy walk weeds and moss, and brighten the gravel, and some people say that salt in the long run feeds the ground and the weeds. I am disposed to think that, in a Little Garden, there is nothing like a weeding woman with an old knife and a little salt afterwards. It is also advisable to be your own weeding woman, that you may be sure that the weeds come up by the roots! Next to the cast-iron back before mentioned, I recommend a housemaid's kneeling mat (such as is used for scrubbing floors), as a gardener's comfort.

I hope, if you have been bulb planting, that you got them all in by Lord Mayor's Day. Whether bulbs should be planted deep or shallow is another "vexed question." In a Little Garden, where you don't want to disturb them, and may like to plant out some small-rooted annuals on the top of them later on, I should plant deep.

If you are planting roses, remember that two or three, carefully planted in good stuff that goes deep, will pay you better than six times the number stuck *into a hole* in cold clay or sand or builders' rubbish, and left to push their rootlets as best they can, or perish in the attempt. Spread out these rootlets very tenderly when planting. You will reap the reward of your gentleness in flowers. Rose roots don't like being squeezed, like a Chinese lady's feet. I was taught this by one who knows,—He has a good name for the briar suckers and sprouts which I hope you carefully cut off from your grafted roses,—He calls it "the old Adam!"

Yours, &c.

LETTER III

"A good rule
Is a good tool."

DEAR LITTLE FRIEND,

January is not a month in which you are likely to be doing much in your Little Garden. Possibly a wet blanket of snow lies thick and white over all its hopes and anxieties. No doubt you made all tidy, and some things warm, for the winter, in the delicious opportunities of St. Luke's and St. Martin's little summers, and, like the amusing American I told you of, "turned away writing *resurgam* on the gatepost."

I write *resurgam* on labels, and put them wherever bulbs lie buried, or such herbaceous treasures as die down, and are, in consequence, too often treated as mere mortal remains of the departed, by the undiscriminating hand of the jobbing gardener.

Winter is a good time to make plans, and to put them down in your Garden-book. Have you a Garden-book? A note-book, I mean, devoted to garden memoranda. It is a very useful kind of commonplace book, and soon becomes as fascinating as autumn and spring catalogues.

One has to learn to manage even a Little Garden chiefly by experience, which is sure teaching, if slow. Books and gardeners are helpful; but, like other doctors, they differ. I think one is often slower to learn anything than one need be, from not making at once for first principles. If one knew more of these, it would be easier to apply one's own experience, and to decide amid conflicting advice.

Here are a few rough-and-ready "first principles" for you.

Hardy flowers in hedges and ditches are partly fed, and are also covered from cold and heat, and winds, and drought, by fallen leaves and refuse. Hardy flowers in gardens have all this tidied away from them, and, being left somewhat hungry and naked in proportion, are all the better for an occasional top-dressing and mulching, especially in autumn. It is not absolutely necessary to turn a flower border upside down and dig it over every year. It may (for some years at any rate), if you find this more convenient, be treated on the hedge system, and *fed from the top*; thinning big clumps, pulling up weeds, moving and removing in detail.

Concentrated strength means large blooms. If a plant is ripening seed, some strength goes to that; if bursting into many blooms, some goes to each of them; if it is trying to hold up against blustering winds, or to thrive on exhausted ground, or to straighten out cramped and clogged roots, these struggles also demand strength. Moral: Plant carefully, support your tall plants, keep all your plants in easy circumstances, don't put them to the trouble of ripening seed (unless you specially want it). To this end cut off fading flowers, and also cut off buds in places where they would not show well when they came out, and all this economized strength will go into the blossoms that remain.

You cannot grow everything. Grow what suits your soil and climate, and the best kinds of these, as well as you can. You may make soil to suit a plant, but you cannot make the climate to suit it, and some flowers are more fastidious about the air they breathe than about the soil they feed upon. There are, however, scores of sturdy, handsome flowers, as hardy as Highlanders, which will thrive in almost any soil, and under all the variations of climate of the British Isles. Some will even endure the smoke-laden atmosphere of towns and town suburbs; which, sooner or later, is certain death to so many. It is a pity that small florists and greengrocers in London do not know more about this; and it would be a great act of kindness to them and to their customers to instruct them. Then, instead of encouraging the ruthless slaughter of primroses, scores and hundreds of plants of which are torn up and then sold in a smoky atmosphere to which they never adapt themselves, these small shopkeepers might offer plants of the many beautiful varieties of poppies, from the grand *Orientalis* onwards, chrysanthemums, stocks, wall-flowers, Canterbury bells, salvias, oenotheras, snapdragons, perennial lobelias, iris, and other plants which are known to be very patient under a long course of soot. Most of the hardy Californian annuals bear town life well. Perhaps because they have only to bear it for a year. *Convolvulus major*—the Morning Glory, as our American cousins so prettily call it— flourishes on a smutty wall as generously as the Virginian creeper.

North borders are safest in winter. They are free from the dangerous alternation of sunshine and frost. Put things of doubtful hardihood under a north wall, with plenty of sandy soil or ashes over their roots, some cinders on that, and perhaps a little light protection, like bracken, in front of them, and their chances will not be bad. Apropos to tender things, if your Little Garden is in a cold part of the British Isles, and has ungenial conditions of soil and aspect, don't try to keep tender things out of doors in winter; but, if it is in the south or west of the British Isles, I should be tempted to very wide experiments with lots of plants not commonly reckoned "hardy." Where laurels flower freely you will probably be successful eight years out of ten. Most fuchsias, and tender things which *die down*, may be kept.

Very little will keep Jack Frost out, if he has not yet been in, either in the garden or the house. A "hot bottle" will keep frost out of a small room where one has stored geraniums, &c., so will a small paraffin lamp (which—N.B.—will also keep water-pipes from catastrophe). How I have toiled, in my young days, with these same hot-water bottles in a cupboard off the nursery, which was my nearest approach to a greenhouse! And how sadly I have experienced that where Mr. Frost goes out Mr. Mould is apt to slink in! Truly, as Mr. Warner says, "the gardener needs all the consolations of a high philosophy!"

It is a great satisfaction if things *will* live out of doors. And in a *little* garden a good deal of coddling may be done. I am going to get some round fruit hampers to turn over certain tender pets this winter. When one has one's flowers by the specimen and not by the score, such cosseting is possible. Ashes and cinders are excellent protection for the roots, and for plants—like roses—which do not die back to the earth level, and which sometimes require a screen as well as a quilt, bracken, fir branches, a few pea-sticks, and matting or straw are all handy helps. The old gentleman who ran out—without his dressing-gown—to fling his own bed-quilt over some plants endangered by an unexpected frost, came very near to having a fine show of bloom and not being there to see it; but, short of this excessive zeal, when one's garden is a little one, and close to one's threshold, one may catch Jack Frost on the surface of many bits of rough-and-ready fencing on very cold nights.

Juliana Horatia Ewing

In drought, one good soaking with tepid water is worth six sprinklings. Watering is very fatiguing, but it is unskilled labour, and one ought to be able to hire strong arms to do it at a small rate. But I never met the hired person yet who could be persuaded that it was needful to do more than make the surface of the ground look as if it had been raining.

There is a "first principle" of which some gardeners are very fond, but in which I do not believe, that if you begin to water you must go on, and that too few waterings do harm. What I don't believe is that they do harm, nor did I ever meet with a gardener who complained of an odd shower, even if the skies did not follow it up. An odd sprinkling does next to no good, but an odd soaking may save the lives of your plants. In very hot weather don't grudge a few waterings to your polyanthuses and primroses. If they are planted in open sunny borders, with no shade or hedge-mulching, they suffer greatly from drought.

Flowers, like human beings, are, to some extent, creatures of habit. They get used to many things which they can't at all abide once in a way. If your Little Garden (like mine) is part of a wandering establishment, here to-day and there to-morrow, you may get even your roses into very good habits of moving good-humouredly, and making themselves quickly at home. If plants from the first are accustomed to being moved about,—every year, or two years,—they do not greatly resent it. A real "old resident," who has pushed his rootlets far and wide, and never tried any other soil or aspect, is very slow to settle elsewhere, even if he does not die of *nostalgia* and nervous shock! In making cuttings, consider the habits and customs of the parent plant. If it has been grown in heat, the cuttings will require heat to start them. And so on, as to dry soil or moist, &c. If somebody gives you "a root" in hot weather, or a bad time for moving, when you have made your hole pour water in very freely. Saturate the ground below, "puddle in" your plants with plenty more, and you will probably save it, especially if you turn a pot or basket over it in the heat of the day. In warm weather plant in the evening, the new-comers then have a round of the clock in dews and restfulness before the sun is fierce enough to make them flag. In cold weather move in the morning, and for the same period they will be safe from possible frost. Little, if any, watering is needed for late autumn plantings.

Those parts of a plant which are not accustomed to exposure are those which suffer from it. You may garden bare-handed in a cold wind and not be the worse for it, but, if both your arms were bared to the shoulders, the consequences would probably be very different. A bundle of rose-trees or shrubs will bear a good deal on their leaves and branches, but for every moment you leave their roots exposed to drying and chilling blasts they suffer. When a plant is out of the ground, protect its crown and its roots at once. If a plant is moved quickly, it is advantageous, of course, to take it up with as much earth as possible, if the roots remain undisturbed in their little plat. Otherwise, earth is no better than any other protection; and in sending plants by post, &c. (when soil weighs very heavily), it is better to wash every bit of soil out of the roots, and then thoroughly wrap them in moss, and outside that in hay or tow, or cotton-wool. Then, if the roots are comfortably spread in nice mould at the other end of the journey, all should go well.

I reserve a sneaking credulity about "lucky fingers." Or rather, I should say, a belief that some people have a strange power (or tact) in dealing with the vegetable world, as others have in controlling and coaxing animals.

It is a vivid memory of my childhood that (amongst the box-edged gardens of a family of eight), that of my eldest brother was almost inconvenienced by the luck of his fingers.

Juliana Horatia Ewing

"Survival of the fittest" (if hardiest does mean fittest!) kept the others within bounds; but what he begged, borrowed, and stole, survived, all of it, conglomerate around the "double velvet" rose, which formed the centre-piece. We used to say that when the top layer was pared off, a buried crop came up.

An old friend with lucky fingers visited my Little Garden this autumn. He wanders all over the world, and has no garden of his own except window-boxes in London, where he seems to grow what he pleases. He is constantly doing kindnesses, and likes to do them his own way. He christened a border (out of which I had not then turned the builders' rubbish) Desolation Border, with more candour than compliment. He said it wanted flowers, and he meant to sow some. I suggested that, sown at that period of the summer, they would not flower this season. He said they would. (They did.) None of my suggestions met with favour, so I became gratefully passive, and watched the lucky fingers from a distance, fluttering small papers, and making mystic deposits here and there, through the length and breadth of the garden. I only begged him to avoid my labels. The seeds he sowed ranged from three (rather old) seeds of bottle gourd to a packet of mixed Virginian stock. They all came up. He said, "I shall put them in where I think it is desirable, and when they come up you'll see where they are." I did.

For some days after his departure, on other country visits, I received plants by post. Not in tins, or boxes, but in envelopes with little or no packing. In this way came sea lavender in full bloom, crimson monkey plant from the London window-box, and cuttings of mesembryanthemum. They are all alive and thriving!

The bottle gourd and the annuals have had their day, and it is over; but in the most unexpected places there still rise, like ghosts, certain plants which completely puzzle me.[4] They have not blossomed, but they grow on in spite of frost. Some of them are nearly as tall as myself. They almost alarm me when I am dividing violas, and trifling with alpines. They stand over me (without sticks) and seem to say, "We are up, you see where we are! We shall grow as long as we think it desirable."

Farewell for the present, Little Friend,

Yours, &c.

[Footnote 4: When fully grown these plants proved to be the Tree-Mallow, *Lavatera arborea*; the seeds were gathered from specimens on the shores of the Mediterranean.]

LETTER IV

"When Candlemas Day is come and gone,
The snow lies on a hot stone."

—Old Saw

DEAR LITTLE FRIEND,

Among all the changes and chances of human life which go
to make up fiction as well as fact, there is one change which
has never chanced to any man; and yet the idea has been
found so fascinating by all men that it appears in the
literature of every country. Most other fancied transfor-
mations are recorded as facts somewhere in the history of
our race. Poor men have become rich, the beggar has sat
among princes, the sick have been made whole, the dead
have been raised, the neglected man has awoke to find
himself famous, rough and kindly beasts have been charmed
by lovely ladies into very passable Princes, and it would be
hard to say that the ugly have not seen themselves beautiful
in the mirror of friendly eyes; but the old have never become
young. The elixir of youth has intoxicated the imagination of
many, but no drop of it has ever passed human lips.

If we ever do just taste anything of the vital, hopeful rapture, the elastic delight of the old man of a fairy tale, who leaves his cares, his crutches, and his chimney-corner, to go forth again young amongst the young,—it is when the winter is ended and the spring is come. Some people may feel this rising of the sap of life within them more than others, but there are probably very few persons whom the first mild airs and bursting buds and pushing flower-crowns do not slightly intoxicate with a sort of triumphant pleasure.

What then, dear little friend, must be the February feelings of the owner of a Little Garden? Knowing, as we do, every plant and its place,—having taken just pride in its summer bloom,—having preserved this by cares and trimmings and proppings to a picturesque and florid autumn, though wild-flowers have long been shrivelled and shapeless,—having tidied it up and put a little something comforting round it when bloom and outline were absolutely no more: what must we feel when we first detect the ruddy young shoots of our favourite paeonies, or perceive that the brown old hepaticas have become green and young again and are full of flower-buds?

The process of strolling, with bent back and peering eyes, by the side of the still frosty borders is so deeply interesting, and a very little sunshine on a broad band of crocuses has such a summer-like effect, that one is apt to forget that it is one of the cheapest ways of catching cold. The last days of the gardening year not unfrequently lead from the flower-bed to the sick-bed. But though there is for susceptible folk a noxious influence in the decaying vegetation of autumn, from which spring is free, there is bitter treachery in many a spring wind, and the damp of the ground seems to reek with the exuding chill of all the frosts that have bound it in mid-winter.

I often wonder that, for some exigencies of weather, the

outdoor red-flannel knickerbockers which one wears in Canada are not more in use here. The very small children have all their clothes stuffed into them, and tumble safely about in the snow like little Dutchmen. Older wearers of petticoats cram all in except the outermost skirt. It is a very simple garment made of three pieces,—two (straight) legs and a large square. The square is folded like a kerchief, and the leg pieces attached to the two sloping sides. A broad elastic and small openings on each side and at the top enable these very baggy knickerbockers to be easily pulled on for going out (where they effectually exclude cold exhalations from snow or damp ground), and pulled off on coming in.

Short of such coddling as this, I strongly urge fleecy cork socks inside your garden boots; and I may add that if you've never tried them, you can have no idea of the warmth and comfort of a pair of boy's common yellow-leather leggings, but the buttons will require some adjusting.

Of course, very robust gardeners are independent of these troublesome considerations; but the gardening members of a family, whether young or old, are very often not those vigorous people who can enjoy their fresh air at unlimited tennis or a real good stretching walk over the hills. They are oftener those weaker vessels who have to be content with strolls, and drives, and sketching, and "pottering about the garden."

Now, pottering about the garden in spring and autumn has many risks for feeble vitalities, and yet these are just the seasons when everything requires doing, and there is a good hour's work in every yard of a pet border any day. So *verbum sap.* One has to "pay with one's person" for most of one's pleasures, if one is delicate; but it is possible to do a great deal of equinoctial grubbing with safety and even benefit, if one is very warmly protected, especially about the feet and legs. These details are very tedious for young people, but not so tedious as being kept indoors by a cold.

And not only must delicate gardeners be cosseted with little advantages at these uncertain seasons, the less robust of the flowers gain equally by timely care. Jack Frost comes and goes, and leaves many plants (especially those planted the previous autumn) half jumped out of the ground. Look out for this, and tread them firmly in again. A shovel-full of cinder-siftings is a most timely attention round the young shoots of such as are poking up their noses a little too early, and seem likely to get them frost-bitten. Most alpines and low-growing stuff will bear light rolling after the frost has unsettled them. This is done in large gardens, but in a Little Garden they can be attended to individually. Give a little protection to what is too forward in growth, or badly placed, or of doubtful hardihood, or newly planted. Roses and hardy perennials can be planted in open weather.

But you will; not really be very busy outside till March, and we are not concerning ourselves with what has to be done "in heat," where a good deal is going on.

Still, in mild climates or seasons (and one must always remember how greatly the British Isles vary in parts, as to climate), the idea of seedlings and cuttings will begin to stir our souls, when February "fills dike," if it is "with black and not with white," *i.e.* with rain and not snow. So I will just say that for a Little Garden, and a mixed garden, demanding patches, not scores of things, you can raise a wonderfully sufficient number of half-hardy things in an ordinary room, with one or two bell-glasses to give the moist atmosphere in which sitting-rooms are wanting. A common tumbler will cover a dozen "seedlings," and there you have two nice little clumps of half-a-dozen plants each, when they are put out. (And mind you leave them space to spread.) A lot of little cuttings can be rooted in wet sand. Hard-wooded cuttings may grow along slowly in cool places; little juicy soft ones need warmth, damp, and quick pushing forward. The very tips of fuchsias grow very easily struck early in wet sand, and will flower the same year. Kind friends will give you these, and if they will also give you "tips" of white, yellow, and blue Marguerites (this last is *Agathea celestis*), these strike as easily as chrysanthemums, and are delightful afterwards to cut from. They are not very tender, though not quite hardy.

For the few pots and pans and boxes of cuttings and seedlings which you require, it is well worth while to get a small stock of good compost from a nursery gardener; leaf mould, peat, and sand, whether for seedlings or cuttings. Always *sink* your pot in a second covering. Either have your pots sunk in a box of sand, which you can keep damp, or have small pots sunk in larger ones. A *great-coat* to prevent evaporation, in some shape, is invaluable.

Yours, &c.,

J.H.E.

GARDEN-LORE

Every child who has gardening tools,
Should learn by heart these gardening rules.

He who owns a gardening spade,
Should be able to dig the depth of its blade.

He who owns a gardening hoe,
Must be sure how he means his strokes to go.

But he who owns a gardening fork,
May make it do all the other tools' work.

Though to shift, or to pot, or annex what you can,
A trowel's the tool for child, woman, or man.

'Twas a bird that sits in the medlar-tree,
Who sang these gardening saws to me.

THE LITTLE GARDENER'S ALPHABET OF PROVERBS.

AUTUMN-SOWN annuals flower soonest and strongest.

What you sow in the spring, sow often and thin.

Juliana Horatia Ewing

BULBS bought early are best chosen.

If you wish your tulips to wake up gay,
They must all be in bed by Lord Mayor's Day.

"Cut my leaves this year, and you won't cut my flowers next year," said the Daffodil to Tabitha Tidy.

CUT a rose for your neighbour, and it will tell two buds to blossom for you.

DON'T let me forget to pray for travellers when I thank Heaven I'm content to stay in my own garden. It is furnished from the ends of the earth.

ENOUGH comes out of anybody's old garden in autumn, to stock a new one for somebody else. But you want sympathy on one side and sense on the other, and they are rarer than most perennials.

FLOWERS are like gentlemen—"Best everywhere."[5]

[Footnote 5: "Clowns are best in their own company, but gentlemen are best everywhere."— *Old Proverb*]

GIVE Mother Earth plenty of food, and she'll give you plenty of flowers.

HE who can keep what he gets, and multiply what he has got, should always buy the best kinds; and he who can do neither should buy none.

IF nothing else accounts for it, ten to one there's a worm in the pot.

JOBBING gardeners are sometimes neat, and if they leave

their rubbish behind them, the hepaticas may turn up again.

KNOWN sorts before new sorts, if your list has limits.

LEAVE a bit behind you—for conscience's sake—if it's only *Polypodium Vulgaris*.

MISCHIEF shows in the leaves, but lies at the root.

NORTH borders are warmest in winter.

OLD women's window-plants have guardian angels.

PUSSY cats have nine lives and some pot-plants have more; but both do die of neglect.

QUAINT, gay, sweet, and good for nosegays, is good enough for my garden.

RUBBISH is rubbish when it lies about—compost when it's all of a heap—and food for flowers when it's dug in.

SOW thick, and you'll have to thin; but sow peas as thick as you please.

TREE-LEAVES in the garden, and tea-leaves in the parlour, are good for mulching.

"USEFUL if ugly," as the toad said to the lily when he ate the grubs.

VERY little will keep Jack Frost out—*before he gets in.*

WATER your rose with a slop-pail when it's in bud, and you'll be asked the name of it when it's in flower.

XERANTHEMUM, Rhodanthe, Helichrysum, white yellow, purple, and red.

> Grow us, cut us, tie us, and hang us with drooping head. Good Christians all, find a nook for us, for we bloom for the Church and the Dead.

YOU may find more heart's-ease in your garden than grows in the pansy-bed.

ZINNIA elegans flore-pleno is a showy annual, and there's a coloured picture in the catalogue; but—like many other portraits—it's a favourable likeness.

SUNFLOWERS AND A RUSHLIGHT

Sunflowers and a Rushlight originally appeared in "Aunt Judy's Magazine," November 1882. It is now re-published for the first time.

CHAPTER I

"A MAN NAMED SOLOMON"—JAEL AND THE CHINA POODLE—JOHNSON'S DICTIONARY— NAIL-SPOTS—FAMILY BEREAVEMENTS—A FAMILY DOCTOR—THE BOOKS IN THE ATTIC— A PUZZLING TALE—"A JOURNEY TO GO."

Doctor Brown is our doctor. He lives in our village, at the top of the hill.

When we were quite little, and had scarlet-fever, and measles, and those things, Dr. Brown used to be very kind to us, and dress his first finger up in his pocket-handkerchief with a knot for the turban, and rings on his thumb and middle finger, and do—"At the top of a hill lived a man named Solomon," in a hollow voice, which frightened me rather.

And then he used to say—"Wise man, Solomon! He lived at

Juliana Horatia Ewing

the top of a hill," and laugh till his face got redder than usual, and his eyes filled with laughter-tears, and twinkled in the nice way they do, and I was not frightened any more.

Dr. Brown left off being our doctor once. That was when he and Grandmamma quarrelled. But they made it up again.

It was when I was so unhappy—I tried to help it, but I really could not—about my poor dear white china poodle (Jael broke him when she was dusting, and then she swept up his tail, though I have so begged her to keep the bits when she cleans our room, and breaks things; and now he never never can be mended, all the days of my life):—it was when I was crying about him, and Grandmamma told Dr. Brown how silly I was, to make me feel ashamed, that he said—"There are some tempers which, if they haven't enough people to love, will love things."

Margery says he did not say *tempers* but *temperaments*. I know it began with temper, because it reminded me of Jael, who said "them tears is all temper, Miss Grace," which was very hard, because she knew—she knew quite well—it was about my poodle; and though accidents will happen, she need not have swept up his tail.

Margery is sure to be right. She always it. Besides, we looked it out in Johnson's Dictionary, which we are rather food of, though it is very heavy to lift. We like the bits out of books, in small print; but I could not understand the bits to the word *temperament*, and I do not think Margery could either, though she can understand much more than I can.

There is a very odd bit to the word *temperamental*, and it is signed *Brown*; but we do not know if that means our Dr. Brown. This is the bit: "That *temperamental* dignotions, and conjecture of prevalent humours, may be collected from spots in our nails, we concede."—*Brown*.

We could not understand it, so we lifted down the other volume (one is just as heavy as the other), and looked out "Dignotion," and it means "distinction, distinguishing mark," and then there is the same bit over again, but at the end is "*Brown's Vulgar Errors.*" And we did not like to ask Dr. Brown if they were his vulgar errors, for fear he should think us rude. I thought we might perhaps ask him if they were his errors, and leave out *vulgar*, which is rather a rude word, but Margery thought it better not, and she is sure to be right. She always is.

But we should have liked to ask Dr. Brown about it, if it had not been rude, because we think a good deal of spots on our nails. All we know about them is that you begin at your thumb, and count on to your little finger, in this way,

"A Gift, a Beau,
A Friend, a Foe,
A Journey to go."

I like having a Beau, or a Friend; Margery likes a Gift, or a Journey to go. We neither of us like having Foes.

And it shows that it does come true, because Margery had a white spot in the middle of her left little finger-nail, just when our father's old friend wrote to Grandmamma, for one of us to go and pay him a visit; and Margery went, because she was the elder of the two.

I do not know how I bore parting with her, except with hoping that she would enjoy herself, for she always had wanted so very much to have a journey to go. But if she had been at home, so that I could have taken her advice, I do not think I should have been so silly about the Sunflowers and the Rushlight.

She says—"You'd have put on your slippers, and had a blanket round you at least. But, oh, my dear Grace, you always are so rash!"

I did not know I was. I thought rash people were brave; and if I had been brave, the Rushlight would never have come out of the roof. Still Margery is sure to be right. I know I am very foolish and lonely without her.

There are only two of us. Our father, and our mother, and our brother, all died of fever, nearly five years ago. We shall never see them again till we go to Paradise, and that is one reason why we wish to try to be good and never to be naughty, so that we may be sure to see them again.

I remember them a little. I remember being frightened by sitting so high up on my father's shoulder, and then feeling so safe when I got into my mother's lap; and I remember Robin's curls, and his taking my woolly ball from me. I remember our black frocks coming in the hair-trunk with brass nails to the seaside, where Margery and I were with our nurse, and her telling the landlady that our father and mother and brother were all laid in one grave. And I remember going home, and seeing the stone flags up in the yard, and a deep dark hole near the pump, and thinking that was the grave; and how Margery found me stark with fright, and knew better, and told me that the grave was in the church-yard, and that this hole was only where workmen had been digging for drains.

And then never seeing those three, day after day, and having to do without them ever since!

But Margery remembers a good deal more (she is three years

older than I am). She remembers things people said, and the funeral sermon, and the books being moved into the attic, and she remembers Grandmamma's quarrel with Dr. Brown.

She says she was sitting behind the parlour curtains with Mrs. Trimmer's Roman History, and Grandmamma was sitting, looking very grave in her new black dress, with a pocket-handkerchief and book in her lap, and sherry and sponge biscuits on a tray on the piano, for visitors of condolence, when Dr. Brown came in, looking very grave too, and took off one of his black gloves and shook hands. Then he took off the other, and put them both into his hat, and had a glass of sherry and a sponge biscuit, so Margery knew that he was a visitor of condolence.

Then he and Grandmamma talked a long time. Margery does not know what about, for she was reading Mrs. Trimmer; but she thinks they were getting rather cross with each other. Then they got up, and Dr. Brown looked into his hat, and took out his gloves, and Grandmamma wiped her eyes with her pocket-handkerchief, and said, "I hope I know how to submit, but it has been a heavy judgment, Dr. Brown."

And Margery was just beginning to cry too, when Dr. Brown said, "A very heavy judgment indeed, Madam, for letting the cesspool leak into the well;" and it puzzled her so much that she stopped.

Then Grandmamma was very angry, and Dr. Brown was angry too, and then Grandmamma said, "I don't know another respectable practitioner, Dr. Brown, who would have said what you have said this morning."

And Dr. Brown brushed his hat the wrong way with his coat-sleeve, and said, "Too true, madam! We are not a body of reformers, with all our opportunities we're as bigoted as most priesthoods, but we count fewer missionary martyrs. The sins, the negligences, and the ignorances of every age have gone on much the same as far as we have been concerned, though very few people keep family chaplains, and most folk have a family doctor."

Then Grandmamma got very stiff, Margery says (she always is rather stiff), and said, "I am sorry, Dr. Brown, to hear you speak so ill of the members of an honourable profession, to which you yourself belong."

And Dr. Brown found out that he had brushed his hat the wrong way, and he brushed it right, and said, "Not at all, Madam, not at all! I think we're a very decent set, for men with large public responsibilities, almost entirely shielded from the wholesome light of public criticism, who handle more lives than most Commanders, and are not called upon to publish our disasters or make returns of our losses. But don't expect too much of us! I say we are not reformers. They rise up amongst us now and again; but we don't encourage them, we don't encourage them. We are a privileged caste of medicine men, whose 'mysteries' are protected by the faith of those to whom we minister, a faith fortified by ignorance and fear. I wish you good-morning, Madam."

Margery has often repeated this to me. We call it "Dr. Brown's Speeches." She is very fond of spouting speeches, much longer ones than Dr. Brown's. She learns them by heart out of history books, and then dresses up and spouts them to me in our attic.

Margery says she did not understand at the time what they were quarrelling about; and when, afterwards, she asked Grandmamma what a cesspool was, Grandmamma was cross with her too, and said it was a very coarse and vulgar word, and that Dr. Brown was a very coarse and vulgar person. We've looked it out since in Johnson's Dictionary, for we thought it might be one of Dr. Brown's vulgar errors, but it is not there.

Margery reads a great deal of history; she likes it; she likes all the sensible books in the attic, and I like the rest, particularly poetry and fairy tales.

The books are Mother's books, they belonged to her father. She liked having them all in the parlour, "littering the whole place," Jael says; but Grandmamma has moved them to the attic now, all but a volume of Sermons for Sunday, and the Oriental Annual, to amuse visitors if they are left alone. Only she says you never ought to leave your visitors alone.

Jael is very glad the books were taken to the attic, because "they gather dust worse than chimney ornaments;" so she says.

Margery and I are very glad too, for we are sent to play in the attic, and then we read as much as ever we like; and we move our pet books to our own corner and pretend they are our very own. We have very cosy corners; we pile up some of the big books for seats, and then make a bigger pile in front of us for tables, and there we sit.

Once Dr. Brown found us. We had got whooping cough, and he had come to see if we were better; and he is very big, and he tramped so heavily on the stairs I did really think he was a burglar; and Margery was a little frightened too, so we were very glad to see him; and when he saw us reading at our tables, he said, "So this is the Attic salt ye season life with, is it?" And then he laughed just as he always does.

There is one story in my favourite Fairy Book which

Juliana Horatia Ewing

Margery likes too; it is called "A Puzzling Tale." I read it to Margery when we were sitting in our tree seat in the garden, and I put my hand over the answer to the puzzle, and she could not guess; and if Margery could not guess, I do not think any one else could.

This is the tale:—"Three women were once changed into flowers, and grew in a field; but one was permitted to go home at night. Once, when day was dawning, and she was about to return to her companions in the field and become a flower again, she said to her husband, 'In the morning come to the field and pick me off my stalk, then I shall be released, and able to live at home for the future.' So the husband went to the field as he was told, and picked his wife and took her home.

"Now how did he know his wife's flower from the other two, for all the three flowers were alike?"

(That is the puzzle. This is the answer:)

"He knew his wife because there was no dew upon her flower."

There is a very nice picture of the three flowers standing stiff and upright, with leaves held out like hands, and large round flower faces, all three exactly alike. I have looked at them again and again, but I never could see any difference; for you can't see the dew on the ones who had been out all night, and so you can't tell which was the one who was allowed to go home. But I think it was partly being so fond of those round flower faces in the Puzzling Tale, that made me get so very very fond of Sunflowers.

We have splendid Sunflowers in our garden, so tall, and with such large round faces!

The Sunflowers were in bloom when Margery went away. She bade them good-bye, and kissed her hands to them as well as to me. She went away in a cab, with her things in the hair trunk with brass nails on the top. She waved her hand to me as long as ever I could see her, and she wagged one finger particularly. I knew which finger it was, and what she meant. It was the little finger with that dignotion on the nail, which showed that she had a journey to go.

Juliana Horatia Ewing

CHAPTER II

ON THE WING—SUNFLOWER SAINTS—DEW-DRENCHED—A BAD NIGHT—A BAD HEADACHE—REGULAR REGIMEN IN GRANDMAMMA'S YOUNG DAYS—TIRED NATURE'S SWEET RESTORER—A SINFUL WASTE OF CANDLE-GREASE.

The Sunflowers were in bloom when Margery went away; and the swallows were on the wing. The garden was full of them all the morning, and when she had gone, they went too. They had been restless for days past, so I dare say they had dignotions of their own, that they had a journey to go as well as Margery.

But when they were gone, and she was gone, the garden felt very lonely. The Sunflowers stretched out their round faces just as if they were looking to see if the cab was coming back; and there was a robin, which kept hopping on and off the pump and peeping about with his eyes, as if he could not imagine what had become of all the swallows.

And Margery's black cat came and mewed to me, and rubbed itself against my pinafore, and walked up and down with me till I went in and got the "Ancient Mariner" and my little chair, and came back and read to the Sunflowers.

Sunflowers are quite as good as dolls to play with. Margery and I think them better in some ways. You can't move them about unless you pick them; but then they will stand of themselves, which dolls will not. You can give them names just as well, and you can teach them lessons just as well. They will grow, which dolls won't; and they really live and die, which dolls don't. In fact, for tallness, they are rather like grown-up people. Then more come out, which is nice; and you see the little Sunflowers growing into big ones, which you can't see with dolls.

We can play a Sunday game with the Sunflowers. We do not have any of our toys on Sunday, except in winter, when we have Noah's Ark. In the summer we may go in the garden between the services, and we always walk up and down together and play with the Sunflowers.

The Sunday Sunflower game is calling them after the black-letter saints in the Kalendar, and reading about them in a very old book—a big one with a black leather binding—in the attic, called *Lives of the Saints*. I read, and then I tell it to Margery as we walk up and down, and say—"This is St. Prisca, this is St. Fabian, this is St. Agnes, this is St. Agatha, and this is St. Valentine"—and so on.

What made us first think of having them for Saints on Sunday, was that the yellow does sometimes look so very like a glory round their faces. We choose by turns which name to give to each, but if there is a very big one with a lot of yellow flaming out, we always called him St. George of England, because there is a very old figure of St. George slaying the Dragon, in a painted window in our Church; and St. George's hair is yellow, and standing out all round; and when the sun shines through the window, so that you can't see his nose and his mouth at all clearly, he looks quite wonderfully like a Sunflower. Then on week-days, the game I like best is pretending that they are women changed into flowers.

They feel so grown up with being so tall, that they are much more like grown-up people turned into flowers than like children. I pretend my doll is my child when I play with her; but I don't think I could pretend a Sunflower was my child;

Juliana Horatia Ewing

and sometimes if Margery leaves me alone with rather big Sunflowers, when it is getting dusk, and I look up at them, and they stare at me with their big faces in the twilight, I get so frightened for fear they should have got leave to go home at night, *and be just turning*, that I run indoors as hard as ever I can.

Two or three times I have got up early and gone out to see if any one of them had no dew; but they have always been drenched, every one them. Dew, thick over their brown faces, and rolling like tears down their yellow glories. I am quite sure that I have never seen a Sunflower yet that had had leave to go home at night, and Margery says the same. And she is certain to know.

I had a very bad night, the night after Margery went away. I was so terribly frightened with being alone in the dark. I know it was very silly, but it was most miserable. I was afraid to go and wake Jael, and I was more afraid of going to Grandmamma, and I was most of all afraid of staying where I was. It seemed to be years and years before the light began to come a little, and the noises left off creaking, and dropping, and cracking, and moving about.

Next day I had a very bad headache. Jael does not like me when I have headaches, because I give trouble, and have to have hot water and mustard for my feet at odd times. Jael does not mind bringing up hot water at night; but she says she can't abide folk wanting things at odd times. So she does not like me when I have headaches; and when I have headaches, I do not much like her. She treads so very heavily, it shakes the floor just as ogres in ogre stories shake the ground when they go out kidnapping; and then the pain jumps in my head till I get frightened, and wonder what happens to people when the pain gets so bad that they cannot bear it any longer.

That morning, I thought I never should have got dressed; stooping and fastening things do make you so very bad. I was very late, and Grandmamma was beginning to scold me, but when she saw I had got a headache she didn't—she only said I looked like a washed-out pocket-handkerchief; and when I could not eat any breakfast, she said I must have a dose of rhubarb and magnesia, and as she had not got any rhubarb left, she sent Jael up to Dr. Brown's to get some.

I did not like having to take rhubarb and magnesia; but I was very glad to get rid of Jael for a bit, though I knew she would hate me for having had to take a message at an odd time. It was her shaking the room when she brought in the urn, and knocking the tongs into the fender with her dress as she went by, that had made me not able to eat any breakfast.

Just as she was starting, Grandmamma beckoned to her to come back, and told her to call at the barber's, and tell him to come up in the afternoon to "thin" my hair.

My hair is very thick. I brush as much out as I can; but I think it only gets thicker and thicker. Grandmamma says she believes that is what gives me so many headaches, and she says it is no use cutting it shorter, for it always is kept cut short; the only way is to thin it, that is, cutting lumps out here and there down to the roots. Thinning does make less of it; but when it grows again it is very difficult to keep tidy, which makes Jael say she "never see such a head, it's all odds and ends," and sometimes she adds—"inside *and* out." Margery can imitate Jael exactly.

When Jael came back, she said Dr. Brown would step down and see me himself. So he came.

Then he felt my pulse and asked me what sort of a night I had had, and I was obliged to tell him, and Grandmamma

Juliana Horatia Ewing

was very much vexed, and made me tell the whole truth, and she said I did not deserve any pity for my headaches when I brought them on myself, which is true.

I think it was being vexed with me that made her vexed with Dr. Brown, when he said rhubarb and magnesia would not do me any good. She said she liked a regular system with the health of young people; and when she and her six sisters were girls they were physicked with perfect regularity; they were bled in the spring, and the fall of the leaf; and had their hair thinned and their teeth taken out, once a quarter, by the advice of their excellent friend and local practitioner, who afterwards removed to London, and became very disting-uished, and had his portrait painted in oils for one of the learned societies. And Grandmamma said she had been spared to survive all her family, and had never had a headache in her life.

Though my head was so bad, I listened as hard as I could to hear what Dr. Brown would say. For I thought—"if he makes one of his speeches, they will quarrel, and he will leave off being our doctor again."

But he didn't, he only said—"Well, well, madam, I'll send the child some medicine. Let her go and lie down at once, with a hot bottle to her feet, and as many pillows as she wants under her head; and don't let a sound reach her for the next three or four hours. When she wakes, give her a basin of bread-and-milk."

So he went away, and presently he came back himself with the medicine. It tasted very nice, and he was very kind; only he made Jael so cross with saying she had not put boiling water in the hot bottle, and sending it down again; and then making her fetch more pillows out of the spare bedroom (Jael does not like odd things any more than odd times). But

I never had such a hot bottle or such a comfortable headache before, and he pulled the blind down, and I went to sleep. At first I dreamt a little of the pain, and then I forgot it, and then slept like a top, for hours and hours.

When I awoke I found a basin of bread-and-milk, with a plate over it to keep it warm, on the rush-bottomed chair by the bed. It hadn't kept it very warm. It made me think of the suppers of the Three Bears in their three basins, and I dare say theirs were rather cold too. Perhaps their Jael boiled their bread-and-milk at her own time, whether they were ready for it or not.

But I think mine must have been like the Little Bear's supper, for I ate it all up.

My head was much better, so I went up to our attic, and got out the Fairy Book, that I might not think too much about Margery, and it opened of itself at the Puzzling Tale. I was just beginning to read it, when I heard a noise under the rafters, in one of those low sort of cupboard places that run all round the attic, where spare boxes and old things are kept, and where Margery and I sometimes play at Voyages of Discovery.

I thought Margery's black cat must be shut up there, but when I went to look, there was another crash, and then the door burst open, and out came Jael, with her cap so crushed that I could not help laughing.

I was glad to see her, for my head was well, so I liked her again, and did not mind her being ogre-footed, and I wanted to know what she was doing; but Jael had not got to like me again, and she spoke very crossly, and said it was more trouble of my giving, and that Dr. Brown had said that I was to have a light in my bedroom till Miss Margery came back—"if ever there was a sinful waste of candle-grease!" and that it wasn't likely the Mistress was going to throw away money on box night-lights; and she had sent the boy to the shop for half-a-dozen farthing rushlights—if they kept them, and if not, for half-a-pound of "sixteen" dips, and had sent her to the attic to find the old Rushlight-tin.

"What's it like, Jael?"

"It's like a Rushlight-tin, to be sure," said Jael "And it's not been used since your Pa and Ma's last illness. So it's safe to be thick with dust, and a pretty job it is for me to have to do, losing the pin out of my cap, and tearing my apron on one of them old boxes, all to find a dirty old Rushlight, just because of *your* whims and fancies, Miss Grace!"

"Jael, I am so sorry for your cap and apron. I will go in and find the Rushlight for you. Tell me, is it painted black, with a lot of round holes in the sides, and a little door, and a place like a candlestick in the middle? If it is, I know where it is."

I knew quite well. It was behind a very old portmanteau, and a tin box with a wig and moths in it, and the bottom part of the shower-bath, just at the corner, which Margery and I call Bass's Straits. So I made a Voyage of Discovery, and brought it out, "thick with dust," as Jael had said.

And Jael took it, and went away very cross and very ogre-footed, with her cap still awry; and as she stumped down the attic-stairs, and kept clattering the Rushlight against the rails, I could hear her muttering—"A sinful waste of candle-grease—whims and fancies—scandilus!"

CHAPTER III

PAIN PAST—A REPRIEVE FROM THE BARBER—
SUNFLOWER SLEEP—LITTLE MICHAELMAS
GOOSE—SNUFFING A RUSHLIGHT—A PURSUIT
OF KNOWLEDGE UNDER DIFFICULTIES—
GRANDMAMMA WITH A WATCHMAN'S RATTLE.

Jael's ogre-footsteps had hardly ceased to resound from the wooden stairs, when these shook again to the tread of Dr. Brown.

He said—"How are you?" and I said—"Very happy, thank you," which was true. For the only nice thing about dreadful pain is that, when it is gone, you feel for a little bit as if you could cry with joy at having nothing to bear.

Then I thanked him for asking Grandmamma to let me have the Rushlight till Margery came home; and he said I ought to be very much obliged to him, for he had begged me off the barber too. So I asked him if he thought my hair gave me headaches, and he felt it, and said—"No!" which I was very glad of. He said he thought it was more what I grew inside, than what I grew outside my head that did it, and that I was not to puzzle too much over books.

I was afraid he meant the Puzzling Tale, so I told him it was very short, and the answer was given; so he said he should like to hear it—and I read it to him. He liked it very much, and he liked the picture; and I told him we thought they were Sunflowers, only that the glory leaves were folded in so oddly, and we did not know why. And he said—"Why, because they're asleep, to be sure. Don't you know that flowers sleep as soundly as you do? *They* don't lie awake in the dark!"

And then he shook with laughing, till he shook the red into his face, and the tears into his eyes, as he always does.

Dr. Brown must know a great deal about flowers, much more than I thought he did; I told him so, and he said, "Didn't think I looked as like a flower sprite as yourself, eh? 'Pon my word, I don't think I'm unlike one of your favourites. Tall, ye know, big beaming face, eh? There are people more unlike a Sunflower than Dr. Brown! Ha! ha! ha!"

He laughed, he always does; but he told me quite delightful things about flowers: how they sleep, and breathe, and eat, and drink, and catch cold in draughts, and turn faint in the sun, and sometimes are all the better for a change ("like Miss Margery," so he said), and sometimes are home-sick and won't settle ("which I've a notion might be one of your follies, Miss Grace"), and turn pale and sickly in dark corners or stuffy rooms. But he never knew one that went home at night.

Except for being too big for our chairs and tables, and for going voyages of discovery, I do think Dr. Brown would make a very nice person to play with; he seems to believe in fancy things, and he knows so much, and is so good-natured. He asked me what flower I thought Jael was like; and when I told him Margery could imitate her exactly, he said he must see that some day. I dared not tell him Margery can do him too, making his speeches in the shovel hat we found in an old old hat-box near Bass's Straits, and a pair of old black gloves of Grandmamma's.

When he went away he patted my head, and said Margery and I must come to tea with him some day, and he would show us wonderful things in his microscope, and if we were very good, a plant that eats meat.

"But most flowers thrive by 'eating the air,' as the Irish say, and you're one of 'em, Miss Grace. Do ye hear? You're not to bury yourself in this attic in the holidays. Run out in the garden, and play with your friends the Sunflowers, and remember what I've told you about their going to sleep and setting you a good example. It's as true as Gospel, and there's many a rough old gardener besides Dr. Brown will tell you that flowers gathered in the morning last longer than those gathered in the evening, because those are fresh after a night's nap, and these are tired and want to rest, and not to be taken into parlours, and kept awake with candles. Good-bye, little Michaelmas Goose!" And away he went, clomping down-stairs, but not a bit like Jael.

When bed-time came I was a good deal tired; but after I got into bed I kept my candle alight for a time, hoping Jael would bring the Rushlight and put it on the floor near Margery's bed, as I had asked her to do. But after a while I had to put out my candle, for Grandmamma is rather particular about it, and then I was so sleepy I fell asleep. I was awakened by a noise and a sort of flashing, and I thought it was thunder and lightning, but it was only Jael; she had come stumping in, and was flashing the Rushlight about before my eyes to see if I was asleep, and when she saw I was, she wanted to take it away again, but I begged and prayed, and then I said Grandmamma had promised, and she always keeps her promises, and I should go and ask her. So at last Jael set it down by Margery's bed, and went away more ogre-footed than ever, grumbling and growling about the waste of candle-grease. But I had got the Rushlight, so I didn't mind; I only hugged my knees, and laughed, and lay down again. And when I heard Jael go stumping up-stairs, I knew that she had waited till her own bed-time to bring the Rushlight, and that was why it was late. And I thought to-morrow I would tell Grandmamma, for she promised, and she always performs. She does not spoil us, we know, but

Juliana Horatia Ewing

she is always fair. Jael isn't, always.

A Rushlight is a very queer thing. It looked so grim as it stood by Margery's bed, in a little round of light; rather like a ruined castle in the middle of a lake in the moonshine. A castle with one big door, and a lot of round windows with the light coming through. They made big spots and patches of light all about the room. I could not shut my eyes for watching them, for they were not all the same shape, and they kept changing and moving; at last they got so faint, I was afraid the Rushlight was going out, so I jumped up and went to see, and I found there was a very big thief in the candle, so I got the snuffers out of my candlestick, and snuffed it, and got into bed again; and now there were beautiful big moons of light all over Margery's bed-valance.

Thinking of the thief in the Rushlight made me think of a thief in a castle, and then of thieves getting into our house, and that if one got in at my window I could do nothing except scream for help, because Grandmamma keeps the Watchman's Rattle under her own pillow, and locks her bedroom door. And then I looked at my window, and saw a bit of light, and it made me quite cold, for I thought it was a burglar's lantern, till I saw it was the moon.

Then I knew how silly I was, and I determined that I would not be such a coward. I determined I would not think of burglars, nor ghosts, nor even Margery.

Margery and I are quite sure that we can think of things, and prevent ourselves thinking of things, by trying very hard. But it is rather difficult.

I tried, and I did. I thought I would think of flowers, and of Dr. Brown, for he is very cheerful to think of. So I thought of Sunflowers, and how they eat the air, and go to sleep at night, and perhaps look like the three women in the Fairy Tale. And I thought I would always pick flowers in the morning now, and never at night, when they want to go to sleep and not to be woke up in a parlour with candles.

And then I wondered: Would they wake with candles if they had begun to go to sleep? Would they wake with a jump, as I did, if Jael flashed the Rushlight in their faces? Would the moon wake them? Were they awake then, that very minute, like me, or asleep, as I was before Jael came in? Did they look like the picture in the Fairy Book, with their glory leaves folded over their faces? If I took a candle now, and held it before St. George of England, looking like that, would he wake with a start, and spread his glory leaves out all round, and stare at me, broad-wide awake?

Then I thought how often I had gone out early, and wet my petticoats, to see if any of them had no dew on their faces, and that I had never gone out at night to see if they looked like the women in the Fairy Tale; and I wondered why I never had, and I supposed it was because I was silly, and perhaps afraid of going out in the dark.

Then I remembered that it wasn't dark. There was a moon: besides my having a Rushlight.

Then I wondered if I was very very silly, and why Dr. Brown had called me a Michaelmas Goose. But I remembered that it must be because to-morrow, was the 29th of September.

Then the stairs clock struck eleven.

I counted all the strokes, and then I saw that the Rushlight was getting dim again, so I got up and snuffed it, and all the moons came out as bright as ever; but I did not feel in the least sleepy.

I did not feel frightened any more. I only wished I knew for certain what Sunflowers look like when they are asleep, and whether you can wake them up with candles. And I went on wondering, and watching the moons.

Then the stairs clock struck a quarter-past eleven, and I thought—"Oh, Grace! If you were not such a coward, if you had jumped up when the clock struck eleven, and slipped down the back-stairs, with the Rushlight in your hands, and unlocked the side-door, you might have run down the grass walk without hurting your feet, and flashed it in the faces of the Sunflowers, and had a good look, and got back to bed again before the clock struck a quarter-past; and then it would have been done, and couldn't be undone, and you would have known whether they look like the picture, and if they wake up with candles, and you never could have unknown. But now, you'll go on putting off, and being frightened about it, and perhaps to-morrow Jael will tell Grandmamma you were asleep, and she won't let you have a Rushlight any more, not even when you are a grown-up young lady; and even when you get married and go away, you may marry a man who won't let you have one; and so you may never never know what you want to know, all because you're a Michaelmas Goose."

Then the Rushlight began to get dim again, so I got up and snuffed it, and it shone out bright, and I thought, "If it was Margery she would do it straight off. I won't be a Michaelmas Goose; I'll go while I'm up, and be back before the stairs clock strikes again, and then it will be done and can't be undone, and I shall know, and can't unknow."

So I took up the Rushlight and went as fast as I could.

I met a black beetle on the back-stairs, which was horrid, but I went on. The side-door key is very rusty and very stiff; I had to put down the Rushlight and use both my hands, and just then the clock struck the half-hour, which was rather a good thing, for it drowned the noise of the lock. It did not take me two minutes to run down the grass path, and there were the Sunflowers.

I did it and it can't be undone, but I don't know what I wanted to know after all, for the moon was shining in their faces, so they may not have been really sound asleep. They are so tall, the Rushlight was too heavy for me to lift right up, so I opened the door and took out the candle, and flashed it in their faces. But they did not take as much notice as I expected. Their glory leaves looked rather narrow and tight, but they were not quite like the flower-women in the picture.

Sunflowers are alive, I know; they look so different when they are dead. And I am sure they go to sleep, and wake up with candles, or Dr. Brown would not have said so. But it is rather a quiet kind of being alive and awake, I think. Something like Grandmamma, when she is very stiff on Sunday afternoon, and goes to sleep upright in a chair, and wakes up a little when her book drops. But not alive and awake like Margery's black cat, which must have heard me open the side-door, and followed me without my seeing it. It did frighten me, with jumping out of the bushes, and looking at me with yellow eyes!

Then I saw another eye. The eye of a moth, who was on one of the leaves. A most beautiful fellow! His coloured wings were rather tight, like the Sunflower's glory leaves, but he was wide awake—watching the candle.

I should have got back to bed quicker if it had not been for Margery's black cat and the night-moths. I wanted to get the cat into the house again, but she would not follow me, and the moths would; and I had such hard work to keep them out

Juliana Horatia Ewing

of the Rushlight.

There was nothing to drown the noise the key made when I locked the side-door again, and when I got to the bottom of the back-stairs, I saw a light at the top, and there was Grandmamma in the most awful night-cap you can imagine, with a candle in one hand, and the watchman's rattle in the other.

CHAPTER IV

HEADS OFF!—JAEL AND MASTER JOHN—FAREWELL—A FRIEND IN NEED—A FREE PARDON.

The worst of it was, I caught such a very bad cold, I gave more trouble than ever; besides Grandmamma having rheumatism in her back with the draught up the back-stairs, and nothing on but her night things and the watchman's rattle. I knew I deserved to be punished, but I did not think my punishment would have been such a terrible one.

I hoped it might have been lessons, or even, perhaps, not having the Rushlight again, but I did not think Grandmamma would think of hurting the Sunflowers.

She waited till I was well enough to go out, and I really began to think she was going to be kind enough to forgive me, with a free forgiveness. But that day she called me to her, and spoke very seriously, and said, that to punish me for my misconduct, and to try and cure me of the babyish nonsense I gave way to about things, she had decided to have all the Sunflowers destroyed at once, and not to have any seed sown for new ones, any more. The gardener was to do it next morning, and I was to be there to see. She hoped it would make me remember the occasion, and teach me better sense for the future.

I should have begged and prayed, but it is no use begging and praying to Grandmamma; Jael attends more to that. There was no comfort anywhere, except in thinking that Margery would be at home in two days, and that I could pour out all my sorrow to her.

As I went crying down the passage I met Jael.

"What's the matter now?" said she.

"Grandmamma's going to have all the Sunflowers killed," I sobbed. "Oh, I wish I'd never gone to look at them with the Rushlight!"

"That's how it is," said Jael sagely, "folks always wishes they'd done different when it's too late. But don't sob your heart out that fashion, Miss Grace. Come into the pantry and I'll give you a bit of cake."

"Thank you, dear Jael, you're very kind, but I don't think I *could* eat cake. Oh, Jael, dear Jael! Do you think she would spare one, just one?"

"That she wouldn't, Miss Grace, so you needn't trouble your head about it. When your grandmamma's made up her mind, there's no one ever I saw can move her, unless it be Dr. Brown. Besides, the missus has never much mattered those Sunflowers. They were your mamma's fancy, and she'd as many whims as you have, and put your grandmamma about a good deal. She was always at your papa to be doing this and that to the place, 'Wasting good money,' as your grandmamma said. Your poor papa was a very easy gentleman. He wanted to please his wife, and he wanted to please his mother. Deary me! I remember his coming to me in this very pantry—I don't know if it would be more than three months afore they were both taken—and, standing there, as it might be you, Miss Grace, and saying—'Jael,' he says, 'this window looks out on the yard,' he says; 'do you ever smell anything, Jael? You are here a good deal.' 'Master John,' I says, 'I thank my Maker, my nose never troubles me; but if it did,' I says, 'I hope I know better than to set *my*self up to smell more than my neighbours.'—'To be sure, to be sure,' he says, looking round in a foolish kind of a way at the sink. Then he says, 'Jael, do you ever taste anything in the water? My wife thinks there's something wrong with the well.' 'Master John,' I says, 'with all respect to your good lady, she disturbs her mind a deal too much with books. An ounce of ex-perience, I says, is worth a pound of book learning; and I'll tell you what my father said to them parties that goes round stirring up stinks, when they were for meddling with his farm-yard. "Let wells alone," he says, "and muck-heaps likewise." And my father passed three-score years and ten, Master John, and died where he was born.' Well-a-day! I see your poor Pa now. He stood and looked as puzzled as a bee in a bottle. Then he says—'Well, Jael, my wife says Sunflowers are good against fevers; and there's no harm in sowing some.' Which he did that very afternoon, she standing by him, with her hand on his shoulder; but, bless ye, my dear! they were took long before the seeds was up. Your mother was a pretty woman, I'll say that for her. You'd never have thought it, to look at her, that she was so fond of poking in dirty places."

"Jael!" I said, "Mamma was right about the smells in the back-yard. Margery and I hold our noses"—"you'd a deal better hold your tongues," interrupted Jael.

"We do, Jael, we do, because I don't like mustard-plasters on my throat, and when the back-yard smells a good deal, my throat is always sore. But oh, Jael! If Sunflowers are good for smells, don't you think we might tell Grandmamma, and she would let us have them for that?"

"She'll not, Miss Grace," said Jael, "so don't worry on. They're ragged things at the best, and all they're good for is to fatten fowls; and I shall tell Gardener he may cut their heads off and throw 'em to the poultry, before he roots up the rest."

I could not bear to hear her, so I went out to bid the Sunflowers good-bye.

I held their dear rough stems, rough with nice little white hairs, and I knew how easily their poor heads would cut off, there is so much pith inside the stems.

I kissed all their dear faces one after another. They are very nice to kiss, especially in the sun, for then they smell honey-sweet, like blue Scabious, and lots of flowers that have not much scent, but only smell as if bees would like them. I kissed them once round for myself, and then once for Margery, for I knew how sorry she would be.

And it was whilst I was holding St. George of England's face in my two hands, kissing him for Margery, that I saw the Dignotion on my middle finger-nail.

A Gift, a Beau, *A Friend!*—

And then it flashed into my mind, all in a moment—"There can be no friend to me and the Sunflowers, except Dr. Brown, for Jael says he is the only person who ever changes Grandmamma's mind."

I dawdled that night when I could not make up my mind about going out with the Rushlight, but I did not wait one minute now. I climbed over the garden wall into the road, and ran as hard as I could run up to the top of the hill, where lived a man—I mean where Dr. Brown lived.

Now, I know that he is the kindest person that ever could be. I told him everything, and he asked particularly about my throat and the smells. Then he looked graver than I ever saw him, and said, "Listen, little woman; you must look out for spots on your little finger-nails. You're going away for a bit, till I've doctored these smells. Don't turn your eyes into saucers. Margery shall go with you; I wish I could turn ye both into flowers and plant ye out in a field for three months! but you are not to give me any trouble by turning home-sick, do you hear? I shall have trouble enough with Grandmamma, though I am joint guardian with her (your dear mother's doing, that!), and have some voice in the disposal of your fates. Now, if I save the Sunflowers, will you promise me not to cry to come home again till I send for you?"

"Shall you be able to change her mind, to let us have Sunflowers sown for next year, too?"

"Yes!"

"Then I promise."

I could have danced for joy. The only thing that made me feel uncomfortable was having to tell Dr. Brown about the spot on my middle finger-nail. He Would ask all about it, and so I let out about Johnson's Dictionary and the Dignotions, and Brown's Vulgar Errors, and I was afraid Margery would say I had been very silly, and let a cat out of a bag.

I hope he was not vexed about his vulgar errors. He only laughed till he nearly tumbled off his chair.

I never did have a spot on my journey-to-go nail, but we went away all the same; so I suppose Dignotions do not always tell true.

When Grandmamma forgave me, and told me she would spare the Sunflowers this time, as Dr. Brown had begged them off, she said—"And Dr. Brown assures me, Grace, that when you are stronger you will have more sense. I am sure I hope he is right."

I hope so, too!

DANDELION CLOCKS

Every child knows how to tell the time by a dandelion clock. You blow till the seed is all blown away, and you count each of the puffs—an hour to a puff. Every child knows this, and very few children want to know any more on the subject. It was Peter Paul's peculiarity that he always did want to know more about everything; a habit whose first and foremost inconvenience is that one can so seldom get people to answer one's questions.

Peter Paul and his two sisters were playing in the pastures. Rich, green, Dutch pastures, unbroken by hedge or wall, which stretched—like an emerald ocean—to the horizon and met the sky. The cows stood ankle-deep in it and chewed the cud, the clouds sailed slowly over it to the sea, and on a dry hillock sat Mother, in her broad sun-hat, with one eye to the cows and one to the linen she was bleaching, thinking of her farm.

Peter Paul and his sisters had found another little hillock where, among some tufts of meadow-flowers which the cows had not yet eaten, were dandelion clocks. They divided them quite fairly, and began to tell each other the time of day.

Little Anna blew very hard for her size, and as the wind blew too, her clock was finished in a couple of puffs. "One, two.

Juliana Horatia Ewing

It's only two o'clock," she said, with a sigh.

Her elder sister was more careful, but still the wind was against them. "One, two, three. It's three o'clock by me," she said.

Peter Paul turned his back to the wind, and held his clock low. "One, two, three, four, five. It's five o'clock by my dandelion—I wonder why the fairy clocks all go differently."

"We blow differently," said his sister.

"Then they don't really tell the time," said Peter Paul.

"Oh yes, they do—the fairy time." And the little girls got more clocks, and turned their backs to the wind in imitation of Peter Paul, and went on blowing. But the boy went up to his mother.

"Mother, why do dandelion clocks keep different time? It was only two o'clock by Anna's, and three o'clock by Leena's, and five by mine. It can't really be evening with me and only afternoon with Anna. The days don't go quicker with one person than another, do they?"

"Drive Daisy and Buttermilk nearer this way," said his mother; "and if you must ask questions, ask your Uncle Jacob."

There was a reason for sending the boy to Uncle Jacob with his difficulties. He had been born after his father's death, and Uncle Jacob had taken up the paternal duties. It was he who had chosen the child's name. He had called him Peter Paul after Peter Paul Rubens, not that he hoped the boy would become a painter, but he wished him to be called after some great man, and—having just returned from Antwerp—the only great man he could think of was Peter Paul.

"Give a boy a great name," said Uncle Jacob, "and if there's any stuff in him, there's a chance he'll live up to it."

This was a kindly way of putting the proverb about giving a dog a bad name, and Uncle Jacob's strongest quality was kindness—kindness and the cultivation of tulips.

He was sitting in the summer-house smoking, and reading over a bulb-list when Peter Paul found him.

"Uncle Jacob, why do dandelion clocks tell different time to different people? Sixty seconds make a minute, sixty minutes make an hour, twenty-four hours make a day, three hundred and sixty-five days make a year. That's right, isn't it? Hours are the same length for everybody, aren't they? But if I got to tea-time when it was only two o'clock with Anna, and went on like that, first the days and then the years would go much quicker with me, and I don't know if I should die sooner,— but it couldn't be, could it?"

"Certainly not," said Uncle Jacob; and he went on with his list. "Yellow Pottebakker, Yellow Tournesol and Yellow Rose."

"Then the fairy clocks tell lies?" said Peter Paul.

"That you must ask Godfather Time," replied Uncle Jacob, jocosely. "He is responsible for the clocks and the hour-glasses."

"Where does he live?" asked the boy.

But Uncle Jacob had spread the list on the summer-house table; he was fairly immersed in it and in a cloud of tobacco smoke, and Peter Paul did not like to disturb him.

"Twenty-five Bybloemens, twenty-five Bizards, twenty-five Roses, and a seedling-bed for first bloom this year."

* * * * *

Some of Uncle Jacob's seedling tulips were still "breeders," whose future was yet unmarked[6] (he did not name them in hope, as he had christened his nephew!) when Peter Paul went to sea.

[Footnote 6: The first bloom of seedling tulips is usually without stripes or markings, and it is often years before they break into stripes; till then they are called breeders, and are not named.]

He was quite unfitted for a farmer. He was always looking forward to what he should do hereafter, or backward to the time when he believed in fairy clocks. Now a farmer should live in the present, and time himself by a steady-going watch with an enamelled face. Then little things get done at the right time, which is everything in farming.

"Peter Paul puzzles too much," said his mother, "and that is your fault, Jacob, for giving him a great name. But while he's thinking, Daisy misses her mash and the hens lay away. He'll never make a farmer. Indeed, for that matter, men never farm like women, and Leena will take to it after me. She knows all my ways."

They were a kindly family, with no minds to make this short life bitter for each other by thwarting, as so many well-meaning relatives do; so the boy chose his own trade and went to sea.

He saw many places and many people; he saw a great deal of life, and came face to face with death more than once, and under strange shapes. He found answers to a lot of the old questions, and then new ones came in their stead. Each year seemed to hold more than a life-time at home would have held, and yet how quickly the years went by!

A great many had gone by when Peter Paul set foot once more upon Dutch soil.

"And it only seems like yesterday that I went away!" said he.

Mother was dead. That was the one great change. Peter Paul's sisters had inherited the farm. They managed it together, and they had divided their mother's clothes, and also her rings and ear-rings, her gold skull-cap and head-band and pins,—the heirlooms of a Dutch farmeress.

"It matters very little how we divide them, dear," Anna had said, "for I shall never marry, and they will all go to your girl."

The elder sister was married and had two children. She had grown up very pretty—a fair woman, with liquid misleading eyes. They looked as if they were gazing into the far future, but they did not see an inch beyond the farm. Anna was a very plain copy of her in body, in mind she was the elder sister's echo. They were very fond of each other, and the prettiest thing about them was their faithful love for their mother, whose memory was kept as green as pastures after rain.

On Sunday Peter Paul went with them to her grave, and then to service. The ugly little church, the same old clerk, even the look of that part of the seat where Peter Paul had kicked the paint off during sermons—all strengthened the feeling that it could only have been a few days since he was there before.

As they walked home he told his sisters about the various religious services he had seen abroad. They were curious to hear about them, under a sort of protest, for they disapproved of every form of worship but their own.

"The music in some of the cathedrals is very beautiful," said Peter Paul. "And the choristers in their gowns, singing as they come, always affect me. No doubt only some are devout at heart, and others careless—which is also the case with the congregation—but outward reverence is, at the lowest, an acknowledgment of what we owe, and for my own part it helps me. Those white figures are not angels I know; but they make one think of them, and I try to be worthier of singing GOD'S praises with them."

There was a little pause, and Leena's beautiful eyes were full of reflections.

Presently she said, "Who washes all the white gowns?"

"I really don't know," said Peter Paul.

"I fancy they don't bleach anywhere as they do in Holland," she continued. "Indeed, Brother, I doubt if Dutchwomen are what they were. No one bleaches as Mother did. Mother bleached beautifully."

"Yes, she bleached beautifully," said Anna.

Peter Paul was only to be three weeks at home before he sailed again; but when ten days were over, he began to think the rest of the time would never come to an end. And this was from no want of love for his sisters, or of respect for their friends. One cannot help having an irritable brain, which rides an idea to the moon and home again, without stirrups, whilst some folks are getting the harness of words on to its back. There had been hours in his youth when all the unsolved riddles, the untasted joys, the great possibilities of even a common existence like his, so pressed upon him, that the shortness of the longest life of man seemed the most pitiable thing about it. But when he took tea with Vrow Schmidt and her daughters, and supper-time would not come, Peter Paul thought of the penance of the Wandering Jew, and felt very sorry for him.

The sisters would have been glad if Peter Paul would have given up the sea and settled down with them. Leena had a plan of her own for it. She wanted him to marry Vrow Schmidt's niece, who had a farm.

"But I am afraid you do not care for young ladies?" said she.

Peter Paul got red

"Vrow Schmidt's niece is a very nice young lady," said he.

He was not thinking of Vrow Schmidt's niece, he was thinking of something else—something for which he would have liked a little sympathy; but he doubted whether Leena could give it to him. Indeed, to cure heartache is Godfather Time's business, and even he is not invariably successful. It was probably a sharp twinge that made Peter Paul say, "Have you never wondered that when one's life is so very short, one can manage to get so much pain into it?"

Leena dropped her work and looked up. "You don't say so?" said she. "Dear Brother, is it rheumatism? I'm sure it must be a dreadful risk being out on the masts in the night air, without a roof over your head. But do you wear flannel,

Peter Paul? Mother was very much troubled with rheumatism latterly. She thought it was the dews at milking time, and she always wore flannel."

"Yes, dear, Mother always wore flannel," said Anna.

Peter Paul satisfied them on this head. He wore flannel, red flannel too, which has virtues of its own.

Leena was more anxious than ever that he should marry Vrow Schmidt's niece, and be taken good care of.

But it was not to be: Peter Paul went back to his ship and into the wide world again.

Uncle Jacob would have given him an off-set of his new tulip—a real novelty, and named—if he had had any place to plant it in.

"I've a bed of breeders that will be worth looking at next time you come home," said he.

Leena walked far over the pastures with Peter Paul. She was very fond of him, and she had a woman's perception that they would miss him more than he could miss them.

"I am very sorry you could not settle down with us," she said, and her eyes brimmed over.

Peter Paul kissed the tears tenderly from her cheeks.

"Perhaps I shall when I am older, and have shaken off a few more of my whims into the sea. I'll come back yet, Leena, and live very near to you and grow tulips, and be as good an old bachelor-uncle to your boy as Uncle Jacob was to me."

"And if a foreign wife would suit you better than one of the Schmidts," said Leena, re-arranging his bundle for him, "don't think we sha'n't like her. Any one you love will be welcome to us, Peter Paul—as welcome as you have been."

When they got to the hillock where Mother used to sit, Peter Paul took her once more into his arms.

"Good-bye, good Sister," he said. "I have been back in my childhood again, and GOD knows that is both pleasant and good for one."

"And it is funny that you should say so," said Leena, smiling through her tears; "for when we were children you were never happy except in thinking of when you should be a man."

"And there sit your children, just where we used to play," said Peter Paul.

"They are blowing dandelion clocks," said Leena, and she called them.

"Come and bid Uncle Peter good-bye."

He kissed them both.

"Well, what o'clock is it?" said he. The boy gave one mighty puff and dispersed his fairy clock at a breath.

"One o'clock," he cried stoutly.

"One, two, three, four o'clock," said the girl. And they went back to their play.

And Leena stood by them, with Mother's old sun-hat on her

young head, and watched Peter Paul's figure over the flat pastures till it was an indistinguishable speck.

He turned back a dozen times to wave his hands to her, and to the children telling the fairy time.

But he did not ask now why dandelion clocks go differently with different people. Godfather Time had told him. He teaches us many things.

THE TRINITY FLOWER

A LEGEND

"Break forth, my lips, in praise, and own
The wiser love severely kind:
Since, richer for its chastening grown,
I see, whereas I once was blind."

—*The Clear Vision*, J.G. WHITTIER

In days of yore there was once a certain hermit, who dwelt in a cell, which he had fashioned for himself from a natural cave in the side of a hill.

Now this hermit had a great love for flowers, and was moreover learned in the virtues of herbs, and in that great mystery of healing which lies hidden among the green things of GOD. And so it came to pass that the country people from all parts came to him for the simples which grew in the little garden which he had made before his cell. And as his fame spread, and more people came to him, he added more and more to the plat which he had reclaimed from the waste land around.

But after many years there came a Spring when the colours

of the flowers seemed paler to the hermit than they used to be; and as Summer drew on, their shapes became indistinct, and he mistook one plant for another; and when Autumn came, he told them by their various scents, and by their form, rather than by sight; and when the flowers were gone, and Winter had come, the hermit was quite blind.

Now in the hamlet below there lived a boy who had become known to the hermit on this manner. On the edge of the hermit's garden there grew two crab trees, from the fruit of which he made every year a certain confection, which was very grateful to the sick. One year many of these crab-apples were stolen, and the sick folk of the hamlet had very little conserve. So the following year, as the fruit was ripening, the hermit spoke every day to those who came to his cell, saying—

"I pray you, good people, to make it known that he who robs these crab trees, robs not me alone, which is dishonest, but the sick, which is inhuman."

And yet once more the crab-apples were taken.

The following evening, as the hermit sat on the side of the hill, he overheard two boys disputing about the theft.

"It must either have been a very big man, or a small boy, to do it," said one. "So I say, and I have my reason."

"And what is thy reason, Master Wiseacre?" asked the other.

"The fruit is too high to be plucked except by a very big man," said the first boy. "And the branches are not strong enough for any but a child to climb."

"Canst thou think of no other way to rob an apple tree but by standing a-tip-toe, or climbing up to the apples, when they should come down to thee?" said the second boy. "Truly thy head will never save thy heels; but here's a riddle for thee:

Riddle me riddle me re,
Four big brothers are we;
We gather the fruit, but climb never a tree.

Who are they?"

"Four tall robbers, I suppose," said the other.

"Tush!" cried his comrade. "They are the four winds; and when they whistle, down falls the ripest. But others can shake besides the winds, as I will show thee if thou hast any doubts in the matter."

And as he spoke he sprang to catch the other boy, who ran from him; and they chased each other down the hill, and the hermit heard no more.

But as he turned to go home he said, "The thief was not far away when thou stoodst near. Nevertheless, I will have patience. It needs not that I should go to seek thee, for what saith the Scripture? *Thy sin* will find thee out." And he made conserve of such apples as were left, and said nothing.

Now after a certain time a plague broke out in the hamlet; and it was so sore, and there were so few to nurse the many who were sick, that, though it was not the wont of the hermit ever to leave his place, yet in their need he came down and ministered to the people in the village. And one day, as he passed a certain house, he heard moans from within, and entering, he saw lying upon a bed a boy who tossed and moaned in fever, and cried out most miserably that his throat was parched and burning. And when the hermit looked upon

Juliana Horatia Ewing

his face, behold it was the boy who had given the riddle of the four winds upon the side of the hill.

Then the hermit fed him with some of the confection which he had with him, and it was so grateful to the boy's parched palate, that he thanked and blessed the hermit aloud, and prayed him to leave a morsel of it behind, to soothe his torments in the night.

Then said the hermit, "My Son, I would that I had more of this confection, for the sake of others as well as for thee. But indeed I have only two trees which bear the fruit whereof this is made; and in two successive years have the apples been stolen by some thief, thereby robbing not only me, which is dishonest, but the poor, which is inhuman."

Then the boy's theft came back to his mind, and he burst into tears, and cried, "My Father, I took the crab-apples!"

And after a while he recovered his health; the plague also abated in the hamlet, and the hermit went back to his cell. But the boy would thenceforth never leave him, always wishing to show his penitence and gratitude. And though the hermit sent him away, he ever returned, saying—

"Of what avail is it to drive me from thee, since I am resolved to serve thee, even as Samuel served Eli, and Timothy ministered unto St. Paul?"

But the hermit said, "My rule is to live alone, and without companions; wherefore begone."

And when the boy still came, he drove him from the garden.

Then the boy wandered far and wide, over moor and bog, and gathered rare plants and herbs, and laid them down near the hermit's cell. And when the hermit was inside, the boy came into the garden, and gathered the stones and swept the paths, and tied up such plants as were drooping, and did all neatly and well, for he was a quick and skilful lad. And when the hermit said,

"Thou hast done well, and I thank thee; but now begone," he only answered,

"What avails it, when I am resolved to serve thee?"

So at last there came a day when the hermit said, "It may be that it is ordained; wherefore abide, my Son."

And the boy answered, "Even so, for I am resolved to serve thee."

Thus he remained. And thenceforward the hermit's garden throve as it had never thriven before. For, though he had skill, the hermit was old and feeble; but the boy was young and active, and he worked hard, and it was to him a labour of love. And being a clever boy, he quickly knew the names and properties of the plants as well as the hermit himself. And when he was not working, he would go far afield to seek for new herbs. And he always returned to the village at night.

Now when the hermit's sight began to fail, the boy put him right if he mistook one plant for another; and when the hermit became quite blind, he relied completely upon the boy to gather for him the herbs that he wanted. And when anything new was planted, the boy led the old man to the spot, that he might know that it was so many paces in such a direction from the cell, and might feel the shape and texture of the leaves, and learn its scent. And through the skill and knowledge of the boy, the hermit was in no wise hindered from preparing his accustomed remedies, for he knew the names and virtues of the herbs, and where every plant grew. And when the sun shone, the boy would guide his master's steps into the garden, and would lead him up to certain flowers; but to those which had a perfume of their own the old man could go without help, being guided by the scent. And as he fingered their leaves and breathed their fragrance, he would say, "Blessed be GOD for every herb of the field, but thrice blessed for those that smell."

And at the end of the garden was set a bush of rosemary. "For," said the hermit, "to this we must all come." Because rosemary is the herb they scatter over the dead. And he knew where almost everything grew, and what he did not know the boy told him.

Yet for all this, and though he had embraced poverty and solitude with joy, in the service of GOD and man, yet so bitter was blindness to him, that he bewailed the loss of his sight, with a grief that never lessened.

"For," said he, "if it had pleased our Lord to send me any other affliction, such as a continual pain or a consuming sickness, I would have borne it gladly, seeing it would have left me free to see these herbs, which I use for the benefit of the poor. But now the sick suffer through my blindness, and to this boy also I am a continual burden."

And when the boy called him at the hours of prayer, paying, "My Father, it is now time for the Nones office, for the marigold is closing," or, "The Vespers bell will soon sound from the valley, for the bindweed bells are folded," and the hermit recited the appointed prayers, he always added,

"I beseech Thee take away my blindness, as Thou didst heal Thy servant the son of Timaeus."

And as the boy and he sorted herbs, he cried,

"Is there no balm in Gilead?"

And the boy answered, "The balm of Gilead grows six full paces from the gate, my Father."

But the hermit said, "I spoke in a figure, my Son. I meant not that herb. But, alas! Is there no remedy to heal the physician? No cure for the curer?"

And the boy's heart grew heavier day by day, because of the hermit's grief. For he loved him.

Now one morning as the boy came up from the village, the hermit met him, groping painfully with his hands, but with joy in his countenance, and he said, "Is that thy step, my Son? Come in, for I have somewhat to tell thee."

And he said, "A vision has been vouchsafed to me, even a dream. Moreover, I believe that there shall be a cure for my blindness."

Then the boy was glad, and begged of the hermit to relate his dream, which he did as follows:—

"I dreamed, and behold I stood in the garden—thou also with me—and many people were gathered at the gate, to whom, with thy help, I gave herbs of healing in such fashion as I have been able since this blindness came upon me. And when they were gone, I smote upon my forehead, and said, 'Where is the herb that shall heal my affliction?' And a voice beside me said, 'Here, my Son.' And I cried to thee, 'Who spoke?' And thou saidst, 'It is a man in pilgrim's weeds, and lo, he hath a strange flower in his hand.' Then said the Pilgrim, 'It is a Trinity Flower. Moreover, I suppose that

Juliana Horatia Ewing

when thou hast it, thou wilt see clearly.' Then I thought that thou didst take the flower from the Pilgrim and put it in my hand. And lo, my eyes were opened, and I saw clearly. And I knew the Pilgrim's face, though where I have seen him I cannot yet recall. But I believed him to be Raphael the Archangel—he who led Tobias, and gave sight to his father. And even as it came to me to know him, he vanished; and I saw him no more."

"And what was the Trinity Flower like, my Father?" asked the boy.

"It was about the size of Herb Paris, my Son," replied the hermit, "But instead of being fourfold every way, it numbered the mystic Three. Every part was threefold. The leaves were three, the petals three, the sepals three. The flower was snow-white, but on each of the three parts it was stained with crimson stripes, like white garments dyed in blood."[7]

[Footnote 7: *Trillium erythrocarpum*. North America.]

Then the boy started up, saying, "If there be such a plant on the earth I will find it for thee."

But the hermit laid his hand on him, and said, "Nay, my Son, leave me not, for I have need of thee. And the flower will come yet, and then I shall see."

And all day long the old man murmured to himself, "Then I shall see."

"And didst thou see me, and the garden, in thy dream, my Father?" asked the boy.

"Ay, that I did, my Son. And I meant to say to thee that it

much pleaseth me that thou art grown so well, and of such a strangely fair countenance. Also the garden is such as I have never before beheld it, which must needs be due to thy care. But wherefore didst thou not tell me of those fair palms that have grown where the thorn hedge was wont to be? I was but just stretching out my hand for some, when I awoke."

"There are no palms there, my Father," said the boy.

"Now, indeed it is thy youth that makes thee so little observant," said the hermit. "However, I pardon thee, if it were only for that good thought which moved thee to plant a yew beyond the rosemary bush; seeing that the yew is the emblem of eternal life, which lies beyond the grave."

But the boy said, "There is no yew there, my Father."

"Have I not seen it, even in a vision?" cried the hermit. "Thou wilt say next that all the borders are not set with hearts-ease, which indeed must be through thy industry; and whence they come I know not, but they are most rare and beautiful, and my eyes long sore to see them again."

"Alas, my Father!" cried the boy, "the borders are set with rue, and there are but a few clumps of hearts-ease here and there."

"Could I forget what I saw in an hour?" asked the old man angrily. "And did not the holy Raphael himself point to them, saying, 'Blessed are the eyes that behold this garden, where the borders are set with hearts-ease, and the hedges crowned with palm!' But thou wouldst know better than an archangel, forsooth."

Then the boy wept; and when the hermit heard him weeping, he put his arm round him and said,

Juliana Horatia Ewing

"Weep, not, my dear Son. And I pray thee, pardon me that I spoke harshly to thee. For indeed I am ill-tempered by reason of my infirmities; and as for thee, GOD will reward thee for thy goodness to me, as I never can. Moreover, I believe it is thy modesty, which is as great as thy goodness, that hath hindered thee from telling me of all that thou hast done for my garden, even to those fair and sweet everlasting flowers, the like of which I never saw before, which thou hast set in the east border, and where even now I hear the bees humming in the sun."

Then the boy looked sadly out into the garden, and answered, "I cannot lie to thee. There are no everlasting flowers. It is the flowers of the thyme in which the bees are rioting. And in the hedge bottom there creepeth the bitter-sweet."

But the hermit heard him not. He had groped his way out into the sunshine, and wandered up and down the walks, murmuring to himself, "Then I shall see."

Now when the Summer was past, one Autumn morning there came to the garden gate a man in pilgrim's weeds; and when he saw the boy he beckoned to him, and giving him a small tuber root, he said,

"Give this to thy master. It is the root of the Trinity Flower."

And he passed on down towards the valley.

Then the boy ran hastily to the hermit; and when he had told him, and given him the root, he said,

"The face of the pilgrim is known to me also, O my Father! For I remember when I lay sick of the plague, that ever it seemed to me as if a shadowy figure passed in and out, and went up and down the streets, and his face was as the face of this pilgrim. But—I cannot deceive thee—methought it was the Angel of Death."

Then the hermit mused; and after a little space he answered,

"It was then also that I saw him. I remember now. Nevertheless, let us plant the root, and abide what GOD shall send."

And thus they did.

And as the Autumn and Winter went by, the hermit became very feeble, but the boy constantly cheered him, saying, "Patience, my Father. Thou shalt see yet!"

But the hermit replied, "My Son, I repent me that I have not been patient under affliction. Moreover, I have set thee an ill example, in that I have murmured at that which GOD—Who knoweth best—ordained for me."

And when the boy ofttimes repeated, "Thou shalt yet see," the hermit answered, "If GOD will. When GOD will. As GOD will."

And when he said the prayers for the Hours, he no longer added what he had added beforetime, but evermore repeated, "If THOU wilt. When THOU wilt. As THOU wilt!"

And so the Winter passed; and when the snow lay on the ground the boy and the hermit talked of the garden; and the boy no longer contradicted the old man, though he spoke continually of the hearts-ease, and the everlasting flowers, and the palm. For he said, "When Spring comes I may be able to get these plants, and fit the garden to his vision."

And at length the Spring came. And with it rose the Trinity Flower. And when the leaves unfolded, they were three, as the hermit had said. Then the boy was wild with joy and with impatience. And when the sun shone for two days together, he would kneel by the flower, and say, "I pray thee, Lord, send showers, that it may wax apace." And when it rained, he said, "I pray Thee, send sunshine, that it may blossom speedily." For he knew not what to ask. And he danced about the hermit, and cried, "Soon shalt thou see."

But the hermit trembled, and said, "Not as I will, but as THOU wilt!"

And so the bud formed. And at length one evening, before he went down to the hamlet, the boy came to the hermit and said, "The bud is almost breaking, my Father. To-morrow thou shalt see."

Then the hermit moved his hands till he laid them on the boy's head, and he said,

"The Lord repay thee sevenfold for all thou hast done for me, dear child. And now I pray thee, my Son, give me thy pardon for all in which I have sinned against thee by word or deed, for indeed my thoughts of thee have ever been tender." And when the boy wept, the hermit still pressed him, till he said that he forgave him. And as they unwillingly parted, the hermit said, "I pray thee, dear Son, to remember that, though late, I conformed myself to the will of GOD."

Saying which, the hermit went into his cell, and the boy returned to the village.

But so great was his anxiety, that he could not rest; and he returned to the garden ere it was light, and sat by the flower till the dawn.

And with the first dim light he saw that the Trinity Flower was in bloom. And as the hermit had said, it was white, and stained with crimson as with blood.

Then the boy shed tears of joy, and he plucked the flower and ran into the hermit's cell, where the hermit lay very still upon his couch. And the boy said, "I will not disturb him. When he wakes he will find the flower." And he went out and sat down outside the cell and waited. And being weary as he waited, he fell asleep.

Now before sunrise, whilst it was yet early, he was awakened by the voice of the hermit crying, "My Son, my dear Son!" and he jumped up, saying, "My Father!"

But as he spoke the hermit passed him. And as he passed he turned, and the boy saw that his eyes were open. And the hermit fixed them long and tenderly on him.

Then the boy cried, "Ah, tell me, my Father, dost thou see?"

And he answered, "*I see now!*" and so passed on down the walk.

And as he went through the garden, in the still dawn, the boy trembled, for the hermit's footsteps gave no sound. And he passed beyond the rosemary bush, and came not again.

And when the day wore on, and the hermit did not return, the boy went into his cell.

Without, the sunshine dried the dew from paths on which the hermit's feet had left no prints, and cherished the Spring flowers bursting into bloom. But within, the hermit's dead body lay stretched upon his pallet, and the Trinity Flower was in his hand.

LADDERS TO HEAVEN

A LEGEND [8]

There was a certain valley in which the grass was very green, for it was watered by a stream which never failed; and once upon a time certain pious men withdrew from the wide world and from their separate homes, and made a home in common, and a little world for themselves, in the valley where the grass was green.

[Footnote 8: "Ladders to Heaven" was an old name for Lilies of the Valley.]

The world outside, in those days, was very rough and full of wars; but the little world in the Green Valley was quiet and full of peace. And most of these men who had taken each other for brothers, and had made one home there, were happy, and being good deserved to be so. And some of them were good with the ignorant innocence of children, and there were others who had washed their robes and made them white in the Blood of the Lamb.

Brother Benedict was so named, because where he came blessings followed. This was said of him, from a child, when the babies stopped crying if he ran up to them, and when on the darkest days old women could see sunbeams playing in his hair. He had always been fond of flowers, and as there were not many things in the Brotherhood of the Green Valley on which a man could full-spend his energies, when prayers were said, and duties done, Brother Benedict spent the balance of his upon the garden. And he grew herbs for healing, and plants that were good for food, and flowers that were only pleasant to the eyes; and where he sowed he reaped, and what he planted prospered, as if blessings followed him.

In time the fame of his flowers spread beyond the valley, and people from the world outside sent to beg plants and seeds of him, and sent him others in return. And he kept a roll of the plants that he possessed, and the list grew longer with every Autumn and every Spring; so that the garden of the monastery became filled with rare and curious things, in which Brother Benedict took great pride.

The day came when he thought that he took too much pride. For he said, "The cares of the garden are, after all, cares of this world, and I have set my affections upon things of the earth." And at last, it so troubled him that he obtained leave to make a pilgrimage to the cell of an old hermit, whose wisdom was much esteemed, and to him he told his fears.

But when Brother Benedict had ended his tale, the old man said, "Go in peace. What a man labours for he must love, if he be made in the image of his Maker; for He rejoices in the works of His hands."

So Brother Benedict returned, and his conscience was at ease till the Autumn, when a certain abbot, who spent much care and pains upon his garden, was on a journey, and rested at the Monastery of the Green Valley. And it appeared that he had more things in his garden than Brother Benedict, for the abbey was very rich, and he had collected far and near. And

Brother Benedict was jealous for the garden of the monastery, and then he was wroth with himself for his jealousy; and when the abbot had gone he obtained leave, and made a pilgrimage to the cell of the hermit and told him all. And the old man, looking at him, loved him, and he said:

"My son, a man may bind his soul with fine-drawn strands till it is either entangled in a web or breaks all bonds. Gird thyself with one strong line, and let little things go by."

And Benedict said, "With which line?"

And the hermit answered, "What said Augustine? 'Love, and do what thou wilt.' If therefore thy labours and thy pride be for others, and not for thyself, have no fear. He who lives for GOD and for his neighbours may forget his own soul in safety, and shall find it hereafter; for, for such a spirit—of the toils and pains and pleasures of this life—grace shall, alike build Ladders unto Heaven."

Then Benedict bowed his head, and departed; and when he reached home he found a messenger who had ridden for many days, and who brought him a bundle of roots, and a written message, which ran thus:

"These roots, though common with us, are unknown where thou dwellest. It is a lily, as white and as fragrant as the Lily of the Annunciation, but much smaller. Beautiful as it is, it is hardy, and if planted in a damp spot and left strictly undisturbed it will spread and flourish like a weed. It hath a rare and delicate perfume, and having white bells on many footstalks up the stem, one above the other, as the angels stood in Jacob's dream, the common children call it Ladders to Heaven."

And when Brother Benedict read the first part of the letter he laughed hastily, and said, "The abbot hath no such lily." But when he had finished it, he said, "GOD rid my soul of self-seeking! The common children shall have them, and not I."

And, seizing the plants and a spade, he ran out beyond the bounds of the monastery, and down into a little copse where the earth was kept damp by the waters of the stream which never failed. And there he planted the roots, and as he turned to go away he said, "The blessing of our Maker rest on thee! And give joy of thy loveliness, and pleasure of thy perfume, to others when I am gone. And let him who enjoys remember the soul of him who planted thee."

And he covered his face with his hands, and went back to the monastery. And he did not enter the new plant upon his roll, for he had no such lily in his garden.

*   *   *   *   *

Brother Benedict's soul had long departed, when in times of turbulence and change the monastery was destroyed, and between fire and plunder and reckless destruction everything perished, and even the garden was laid waste. But no one touched the Lilies of the Valley in the copse below, for they were so common that they were looked upon as weeds. And though nothing remained of the brotherhood but old tales, these lingered, and were handed on; and when the children played with the lilies and bickered over them, crying, "My ladder has twelve white angels and yours has only eight," they would often call them Brother Benedict's flowers, adding, "but the real right name of them is Ladders to Heaven."

And after a time a new race came into the Green Valley and filled it; and the stream which never failed turned many wheels, and trades were brisk, and they were what are called black trades. And men made money soon, and spent it soon, and died soon; and in the time between each lived for himself, and had little reverence for those who were gone, and less concern for those who should come after. And at first they were too busy to care for what is only beautiful, but after a time they built smart houses, and made gardens, and went down into the copse and tore up clumps of Brother Benedict's flowers, and planted them in exposed rockeries, and in pots in dry hot parlours, where they died, and then the good folk went back for more; and no one reckoned if he was taking more than his fair share, or studied the culture of what he took away, or took the pains to cover the roots of those he left behind, and in three years there was not left a Ladder to Heaven in all the Green Valley.

*   *   *   *   *

The Green Valley had long been called the Black Valley, when those who laboured and grew rich in it awoke—as man must sooner or later awake—to the needs of the spirit above the flesh. They were a race famed for music, and they became more so. The love of beauty also grew, and was cultivated, and in time there were finer flowers blossoming in that smoky air than under many brighter skies. And with the earnings of their grimy trades they built a fine church, and adorned it more richly than the old church of the monastery that had been destroyed.

The parson who served this church and this people was as well-beloved by them as Brother Benedict had been in his day, and it was in striving to link their minds with sympathies of the past as well as hopes of the future, that one day he told them the legend of the Ladders to Heaven. A few days afterwards he was wandering near the stream, when he saw two or three lads with grimy faces busily at work in the wood through which the stream ran. At first, when he came suddenly on them, they looked shyly at one another, and at last one stood up and spoke.

"It's a few lily roots, sir, we got in the market, and we're planting them; and two or three of us have set ourselves to watch that they are not shifted till they've settled. Maybe we shall none of us see them fair wild here again, any more than Brother Benedict did. For black trades are short-lived trades, and there's none of us will be as old as he. But maybe we can take a pride too in thinking that they'll blow for other folk and other folk's children when we are gone."

* * * * *

Once more the fastidious[9] flowers spread, and became common in the valley, and were guarded with jealous care; and the memory of Brother Benedict lingered by the stream, and was doubly blessed.

[Footnote 9: It is well known that Lilies of the Valley are flowers which resent disturbance, though they are perfectly hardy and vigorous if left in peace.]

For if he is blessed whose love and wisdom add to the world's worth, and make life richer in pleasant things, thrice blessed is he whose unselfish example shall be culture to the ignorant or the thoughtless, and set Ladders to Heaven for the feet of those who follow him!

THE END

Juliana Horatia Ewing

ABOUT THE AUTHOR

 **Mrs. Juliana Horatia Ewing** (née Gatty) (1841–1885) was a writer of children's stories, daughter of The Rev. Alfred Gatty and Margaret Gatty, also a writer for children. Among her tales, which have hardly been excelled in sympathetic insight into child-life, and still enjoy undiminished popularity, are: Mrs. Overtheway's Remembrances (1869), A Flat Iron for a Farthing (1872), Six to Sixteen (1875), Jan of the Windmill (1876), Jackanapes (1884), and The Story of a Short Life (1885).

Her works have been called the "first outstanding child-novels" in English literature.[1]

She was born at Ecclesfield, Yorkshire on August 3, 1841; married June 1, 1867, to Alexander Ewing and died at Bath, May 13, 1885. She was buried at Trull, Somerset, on May 16, 1885.

Other books by this author

A Flat Iron for a Farthing

A Great Emergency and Other Tales

Jan of the Windmill

Melchior's Dream and Other Tales

Miscellanea

Mrs. Overtheway's Remembrances

Brothers of Pity and Other Tales of Beasts and Men

Juliana Horatia Ewing

Choose from Thousands of 1stWorldLibrary Classics By

A. M. Barnard
Ada Leverson
Adolphus William Ward
Aesop
Agatha Christie
Alexander Aaronsohn
Alexander Kielland
Alexandre Dumas
Alfred Gatty
Alfred Ollivant
Alice Duer Miller
Alice Turner Curtis
Alice Dunbar
Allen Chapman
Alleyne Ireland
Ambrose Bierce
Amelia E. Barr
Amory H. Bradford
Andrew Lang
Andrew McFarland Davis
Andy Adams
Angela Brazil
Anna Alice Chapin
Anna Sewell
Annie Besant
Annie Hamilton Donnell
Annie Payson Call
Annie Roe Carr
Annonaymous
Anton Chekhov
Archibald Lee Fletcher
Arnold Bennett
Arthur C. Benson
Arthur Conan Doyle
Arthur M. Winfield
Arthur Ransome
Arthur Schnitzler
Arthur Train
Atticus
B.H. Baden-Powell
B. M. Bower
B. C. Chatterjee
Baroness Emmuska Orczy
Baroness Orczy
Basil King
Bayard Taylor
Ben Macomber
Bertha Muzzy Bower
Bjornstjerne Bjornson

Booth Tarkington
Boyd Cable
Bram Stoker
C. Collodi
C. E. Orr
C. M. Ingleby
Carolyn Wells
Catherine Parr Traill
Charles A. Eastman
Charles Amory Beach
Charles Dickens
Charles Dudley Warner
Charles Farrar Browne
Charles Ives
Charles Kingsley
Charles Klein
Charles Hanson Towne
Charles Lathrop Pack
Charles Romyn Dake
Charles Whibley
Charles Willing Beale
Charlotte M. Braeme
Charlotte M. Yonge
Charlotte Perkins Stetson
Clair W. Hayes
Clarence Day Jr.
Clarence E. Mulford
Clemence Housman
Confucius
Coningsby Dawson
Cornelis DeWitt Wilcox
Cyril Burleigh
D. H. Lawrence
Daniel Defoe
David Garnett
Dinah Craik
Don Carlos Janes
Donald Keyhoe
Dorothy Kilner
Dougan Clark
Douglas Fairbanks
E. Nesbit
E. P. Roe
E. Phillips Oppenheim
E. S. Brooks
Earl Barnes
Edgar Rice Burroughs
Edith Van Dyne
Edith Wharton

Edward Everett Hale
Edward J. O'Biren
Edward S. Ellis
Edwin L. Arnold
Eleanor Atkins
Eleanor Hallowell Abbott
Eliot Gregory
Elizabeth Gaskell
Elizabeth McCracken
Elizabeth Von Arnim
Ellem Key
Emerson Hough
Emilie F. Carlen
Emily Bronte
Emily Dickinson
Enid Bagnold
Enilor Macartney Lane
Erasmus W. Jones
Ernie Howard Pie
Ethel May Dell
Ethel Turner
Ethel Watts Mumford
Eugene Sue
Eugenie Foa
Eugene Wood
Eustace Hale Ball
Evelyn Everett-green
Everard Cotes
F. H. Cheley
F. J. Cross
F. Marion Crawford
Fannie E. Newberry
Federick Austin Ogg
Ferdinand Ossendowski
Fergus Hume
Florence A. Kilpatrick
Fremont B. Deering
Francis Bacon
Francis Darwin
Frances Hodgson Burnett
Frances Parkinson Keyes
Frank Gee Patchin
Frank Harris
Frank Jewett Mather
Frank L. Packard
Frank V. Webster
Frederic Stewart Isham
Frederick Trevor Hill
Frederick Winslow Taylor

Friedrich Kerst	Hayden Carruth	James Branch Cabell
Friedrich Nietzsche	Helent Hunt Jackson	James DeMille
Fyodor Dostoyevsky	Helen Nicolay	James Joyce
G.A. Henty	Hendrik Conscience	James Lane Allen
G.K. Chesterton	Hendy David Thoreau	James Lane Allen
Gabrielle E. Jackson	Henri Barbusse	James Oliver Curwood
Garrett P. Serviss	Henrik Ibsen	James Oppenheim
Gaston Leroux	Henry Adams	James Otis
George A. Warren	Henry Ford	James R. Driscoll
George Ade	Henry Frost	Jane Abbott
Geroge Bernard Shaw	Henry James	Jane Austen
George Cary Eggleston	Henry Jones Ford	Jane L. Stewart
George Durston	Henry Seton Merriman	Janet Aldridge
George Ebers	Henry W Longfellow	Jens Peter Jacobsen
George Eliot	Herbert A. Giles	Jerome K. Jerome
George Gissing	Herbert Carter	Jessie Graham Flower
George MacDonald	Herbert N. Casson	John Buchan
George Meredith	Herman Hesse	John Burroughs
George Orwell	Hildegard G. Frey	John Cournos
George Sylvester Viereck	Homer	John F. Kennedy
George Tucker	Honore De Balzac	John Gay
George W. Cable	Horace B. Day	John Glasworthy
George Wharton James	Horace Walpole	John Habberton
Gertrude Atherton	Horatio Alger Jr.	John Joy Bell
Gordon Casserly	Howard Pyle	John Kendrick Bangs
Grace E. King	Howard R. Garis	John Milton
Grace Gallatin	Hugh Lofting	John Philip Sousa
Grace Greenwood	Hugh Walpole	John Taintor Foote
Grant Allen	Humphry Ward	Jonas Lauritz Idemil Lie
Guillermo A. Sherwell	Ian Maclaren	Jonathan Swift
Gulielma Zollinger	Inez Haynes Gillmore	Joseph A. Altsheler
Gustav Flaubert	Irving Bacheller	Joseph Carey
H. A. Cody	Isabel Cecilia Williams	Joseph Conrad
H. B. Irving	Isabel Hornibrook	Joseph E. Badger Jr
H. C. Bailey	Israel Abrahams	Joseph Hergesheimer
H. G. Wells	Ivan Turgenev	Joseph Jacobs
H. H. Munro	J. G.Austin	Jules Vernes
H. Irving Hancock	J. Henri Fabre	Julian Hawthrone
H. R. Naylor	J. M. Barrie	Julie A Lippmann
H. Rider Haggard	J. M. Walsh	Justin Huntly McCarthy
H. W. C. Davis	J. Macdonald Oxley	Kakuzo Okakura
Haldeman Julius	J. R. Miller	Karle Wilson Baker
Hall Caine	J. S. Fletcher	Kate Chopin
Hamilton Wright Mabie	J. S. Knowles	Kenneth Grahame
Hans Christian Andersen	J. Storer Clouston	Kenneth McGaffey
Harold Avery	J. W. Duffield	Kate Langley Bosher
Harold McGrath	Jack London	Kate Langley Bosher
Harriet Beecher Stowe	Jacob Abbott	Katherine Cecil Thurston
Harry Castlemon	James Allen	Katherine Stokes
Harry Coghill	James Andrews	L. A. Abbot
Harry Houidini	James Baldwin	L. T. Meade